Dada was not only a series of art-historical events which took place between 1916 and 1923, it was, and indeed still is, an emotional, social and political condition. Kenneth Coutts-Smith, lecturer, critic and art historian, charts the phenomenon from its sudden anarchic inception in Zürich when a group of young *émigré* artists reacted violently to the brutality of the first world war, to the present, when its influence can be seen lurking behind so many manifestations of the plastic arts.

With the collapse of pre-1914 social values the Dadaists reacted with ironic, anarchistic and frequently nihilistic gestures, but they also evolved techniques and attitudes that have become central to our aesthetic sensibility. The discovery of automatism in the arts, the use of random elements, and the conclusion that art is not defined by any specific content or material is at the core of much painting and sculpture being produced today, as is also the concept, developed by the Dadaists, that the work of art is 'situational', the result of the confrontation between spectator and object.

The author discusses the Dada movement as it appears in the Zürich group with their debt to Futurism; New York with special reference to the philosophical irony of Duchamp; Berlin with the political activities of Huelsenbeck and Heartfield; Max Ernst in Cologne; Kurt Schwitters in Hanover, and the Littérature group in Paris. He also examines the Neo-Dada revival in the 1950s in Paris and New York, and present-day work in the Dada spirit. The 120 illustrations display Dada in all its aspects.

Himself a painter, Kenneth Coutts-Smith has also published art criticism in many different journals, and was Associate Editor of *Art and Artists* until 1967. His study of art and society in the twentieth century, *The Dream of Icarus*, was published at the beginning of 1970, and he is at present writing a book about art and revolution.

D1245769

```
papa dada nana baba caca vava
     papa dada nana baba caca vava
          vava caca baba nana dada papa
               caca baba nana dada papa vava
               nana baba caca vava papa dada
                    dada papa vava caca baba nana
                    dada
                    papa
                    vava
                    caca
                    baba
                    nana
                    nana                              D
                    baba
A                   caca                              A
                    vava
P                   papa                              D
A                   dada
P                   gaga                              A
A                   gaga
                    gaga
                    gaga
                    dada
                    dada
                    gaga
                    gaga
                    gaga
                    dada papa vava caca baba nana
               nana baba caca vava papa dada
          caca baba nana dada papa vava
     vava caca baba nana dada papa
     papa dada nana baba caca vava
papa dada nana baba caca vava


                                                  dada


hommage à dada par hache see, dit chopin        dada
```

**Henri Chopin** *Hommage à Dada* 1965

# DADA

**Kenneth Coutts-Smith**

**studio vista | dutton pictureback**

general editor David Herbert

## Acknowledgments

The author wishes to extend grateful thanks to Mr Bernard Karpel, Mr George Riabov and Mrs Semmler of the Library of the Museum of Modern Art, New York, for their invaluable help during research for this book. The author's gratitude is also extended to Mr Timothy Baum who has kindly allowed the reproduction of many works from his private collection, as it is also for the same reason to Sir Roland Penrose, Mr Simon Watson-Taylor, Mr Eric Estorick, Mrs Annely Juda, and to the various museums and private galleries who have generously assisted with visual material.

Illustrations on pages 44 and 94, photographs by Deste Photography; pages 8, 10, 12–13, 85, 114–15, 142, 146, 147, Nathan Rabin Photography; pages 50, 52, 53, 58, 60, 61, 63, 125, A. J. Wyatt; pages 42–3, photograph Manuel Bidermanas; page 152, Dick Higgins; page 41, Peter Hirst-Smith; page 109, J. S. Lewinski; page 162, Allan Palmer.

Published in Great Britain by Studio Vista Limited
Blue Star House, Highgate Hill, London N19
and in the USA by E. P. Dutton and Co. Inc.
201 Park Avenue South, New York, NY 10003
Set in 8 on 11 pt Univers 689
Made and printed in Great Britain by
Richard Clay (The Chaucer Press) Ltd, Bungay, Suffolk

SBN 289 79677 6 (paperback)
    289 79678 4 (hardback)

# Contents

GALERIE
CORRAY
BAHNHOFSTR.19.
TIEFENHOFE 12.
1re EXPOSI-
TION·DADA
CUBISTES·ARTNEGRE
OUVERT·10-12·2-6
CONFÉRENCES
SUR L'ART FAITES PAR
TRISTAN·TZARA
SAMEDI·LE 13-20-27 JAN·ENTRÉE 1F

## Zürich—the beginning

During the spring of 1916 the provincial inhabitants of Zürich were amused, astonished, disturbed, even outraged, by the activities of a group of extraordinary young men and women who had suddenly appeared in their midst. The originator of all this uproar was a young *émigré* from war-time Berlin, called Hugo Ball, who had turned up in Switzerland with his mistress Emmy Hennings about a year previously. Before leaving Berlin, Ball has already made a mark upon the intellectual life of the German capital as a poet and theatre director, and was a conspicuous figure among a group of writers, artists and intellectuals who frequented the Café des Westerns, and for whom Emmy, poet herself, cabaret dancer and singer, acted as a sort of popularly elected 'muse'.

On 2 February 1916, several newspapers in Zürich printed the following advertisement:

Cabaret Voltaire. Under this name a group of young artists and writers has formed with the object of becoming a centre for artistic entertainment. The Cabaret Voltaire will be run on the principle of daily meetings where visiting artists will perform their music and poetry. The young artists of Zürich are invited to bring along their ideas and contributions.

It was the announcement of not only a new intellectual and social force but also a new concept of the artist's activity and his role in society. The Cabaret Voltaire constituted the original archetype of both the 'total' art of today's Happening and the young artist's opposition of militaristic and authoritarian assumptions in society.

The very beginnings of the Cabaret Voltaire were comparatively calm and conventional; the early manifestations were mainly literary. Modern Russian, French and German poetry was read, and the music that was played was in the 'modern' impressionistic tradition. Very quickly, however, the group of extremely talented young artists who had gravitated together began to spark each other off. Most of them were refugees from the war that was then raging across the Continent: Ball, Richard Huelsenbeck and Hans Richter from Germany, Hans Arp from France,

**Marcel Janco** Poster for the 1st Dada Exhibition 1917
Collection Timothy Baum, New York

## SALIVE AMÉRICAINE

*L'estomac domino mécanique*
*des bedaines brouillard-*
*bavarde au pas de course poussière*
*et subit la sécheresse du sherry en ballon.*
*Un radis fantastique se cabre*
*en leçon de bouteille*
*auprès de la traile téléphone.*
*Sur un carnet de poche Zanzibar*
*le ni vient sans moyens de transport.*
*Cela me rappelle les nœuds de cravates*
*seuls en wagon.*
*L'escalier tunis avec le bec de gaz*
*mes frères!*

FRANCIS PICABIA

*Bois de E. PRAMPOLINI*

## LA JOIE DES SEPT COULEURS
*(Fragment)*

C'est un homme enfermé dans une projection
basile et hal demande un gui dans la rue et et
Elles sont deux mais il n'y en a qu'une
A Bondelik comme hommes encore fait le pour etre gueur
Bock, Bock, Bock, pas, pas, pas, las, las, las, bac
Ma, ma, ma
Un vautre est passé en causant de sentiment de
Nom du prophétie et déjà vous nous nous rencontrerons
C'est physiologique et cela avec sa proportion
Et il faut que les néants sont raison tumultueux
Nous les tous ces tes sont sont sont mords mords mords
Personne n'a plus obligée de devenir quelquechose
Maison là parti comme voyageur le serpent
Noise et blanc le projecteur est un tumultueux brouillard

PIERRE ALBERT-BIROT

**"SIC"**
(Sons Idées couleurs)
Revue d'art et de littérature
Directeur: P. A. Birot
Paris, 37 rue de la Tombe-Issoire

---

# FLAMME

**Une enveloppe déchirée aggrandit ma chambre**
**Je bouscule mes souvenirs**
**On part**

**J'avais oublié ma valise**

**PHILIPPE SOUPAULT**

## MŌRAR

Altipiano. Collinette nuovi come seni di fanciulla. Se
laggiù, degli alberelli verdegialli disposti curiosamente su qui
cinque file. Cascinali sbiodati allegri.

All'alba si cammina sulla carta vetrata. Aghi rilucenti di v
permuta. Ogni pozzanghera una lastra. Povere di vetro imbio
e irrigidirsi l'erba. Tutto cigola e brilla.

Alla carezza del sole la conca si distende in una beatitu
celma. Si acumula la luna con una morbidità trasparente.

Il brusarsi ne fa un quadro futurista. Penellate giustapp
senza passaggi. Batticieni di arancione di viola cupo, d'arch
che tono i tocchi lontani; intrecciti da chiazze abbaglianti
clone servate.

Più tardi i colori si fondono. Il cielo si sbava di viola
prezonizzonti d'oro. Armonie rauroma che l'occhio soglie con
premura delle gioie uniche e intrasmessibili. Delicatezze, iridesce
da bolle di sapone. A momenti si vive in un vetro soffiato

Infine la nebbiolina smorza l'altipiano nel rugo. Isolotti et a
fragano i cascinali. La luna è un imbuto celestino e la r
contagiosa crea al paesaggio un'atmosfera irreale.

Sorbero galleggio in questa lacerna.

(La guerra dov'è ?)

Camillo Sbarb

Tristan Tzara and the two brothers Georges and Marcel Janco from Rumania, Walter Serner from Austria.

At first the Cabaret Voltaire was fuelled, as it were, by the already existing international movements in modern art. Cubism, and even more spectacularly Futurism, had exploded some seven years previously in the apparently calm pastures of the art world. Futurism, as we shall see, detonated the Dada imagination; and it was this specific Italian artistic anarchism, together with German Expressionism, Parisian Cubism and post-Symbolist poetry, which constituted the programme of the Zürich period. The individual members of the Voltaire group each contributed a direct link with *avant-garde* movements elsewhere. Hans Arp, for instance, had been in close contact with Picasso, Braque and the sources of Cubism; Hugo Ball was a friend of Kandinsky and had once attempted to found together with him an Expressionist theatre in Munich; Jawlensky and Arthur Segal were immersed in the Russian and Central European experiments in pure colour and chromatic relationships; Tristan Tzara provided the line of communication with Futurism, keeping up a long correspondence with the main Italian theoretician, Marinetti.

Tzara was the creative centre of gravity of the group. The mercurial, irreverent and wildly imaginative genius of the Rumanian poet was to provide the impetus for many Dada manifestations and attitudes. He introduced concepts from the Futurists which were to become central to the Dada canon, concepts such as 'simultaneity' and 'bruitism' or noise-music; but it was finally his talent for provocation that was outstanding, his masterly, witty and outrageous manner of undermining his audience, his manifestos and statements with which he tirelessly promoted the cause of Dada, first in Zürich, then later in Paris.

Six months after the founding of the Cabaret Voltaire, a specific mental climate, a certain attitude that went far beyond purely aesthetic questions, began to jell. On 14 July 1916 the first real Dada 'soirée' inaugurated a series of distinctive manifestations; the intense conversations, the wit, nonsense, irony and nihilism which had sparkled across café tables, in hotel bedrooms and studios for months, began to form itself into a particular point of view. On that evening Tzara's public recitation of 'The Manifesto

*On pages 12 and 13*
*Dada* no. 3 1918 double page
Collection Timothy Baum, New York

Bois de H. Arp.

## GUILLAUME APOLLINAIRE

Sa mort me semble encore impossible. Guillaume Apollinaire est un des rares qui ont suivi toute l'évolution de l'art moderne et l'ont complètement comprise, il l'a défendue vaillament et honnêtement parce qu'il l'aimait, comme il aimait la vie, et toutes les formes nouvelles d'activité. Son esprit était riche, somptueux même, souple, sensible, orgueilleux et enfantin. Son œuvre est pleine de variété, d'esprit et d'invention.

*Francis Picabia.*

## circuit total par la lune et par la couleur
## à marcel janco

l'œil de fer en or changera
les boussoles ont fleuri nos tympans
regardez monsieur janco pour la prière fabuleuse
tropical
sur le violon de la tour eiffel et sonneries d'étoiles
les olives gonflent pac pac et se cristalliseront symétriquement
partout
citron
la pièce de dix sous
les dimanches ont caressé lumineusement dieu dada danse
partageant les céréales
la pluie
journal
vers le nord
lentement  lentement
les papillons de 5 mètres de longuer se cassent comme les miroirs
comme le vol des fleuves nocturnes grimpent avec le feu vers la
voie lactée
les routes de lumière la chevelure les pluies irrégulières
et les kiosques artificiels qui volent veillent dans ton cœur quand
tu penses je vois
matinal
qui crie
les cellules se dilatent
les ponts s'allongent et se lèvent en air pour crier
autour des pôles magnétiques les rayons se rangent comme les
plumes des paons
boréal
et les cascades voyez-vous? se rangent dans leur propre lumière
au pôle nord un paon énorme déploiera lentement le soleil
à l'autre pôle on aura la nuit des couleurs qui mangent les serpents
glisse jaune
les cloches
nerveux
pour l'éclaircir les rouges marcheront
quand je demande comment
les fosses hurlent
seigneur ma géométrie

**tristan tzara**

Fr. Picabia : L'athlète des Pompes funèbres " (Poème) Prix 2,50 fr.  En vente au Mouvement Dada.

Gravure originale de MARCEL JANCO.

**Hans Arp** *The Sea* from '7 Arpaden', a portfolio of 7 prints 1923 lithograph
17¾ × 13¾ in.
Museum of Modern Art, New York, gift of J.B.Neumann

of Monsieur Antipyrene', a name taken in deadpan irony from a popular brand of medicine which was also punningly translated as 'Mr Fire-extinguisher', put, in the words of the French critic José Pierre, '. . . an accent on a climate of chaos, of disorder and vehement contradictions through which Dada undertook to negate the established order'.

The events proliferated. A theatrical group appeared, the Laban Dance Theatre, whose revolutionary choreography was to

**Hans Arp** *Arabian Eight* from '7 Arpaden' 1923 lithograph $17\frac{3}{4} \times 13\frac{3}{4}$ in.
Museum of Modern Art, New York, gift of J.B.Neumann

be influential in the modern ballet, and for whose performances
Max Oppenheimer and Janco created masks while Richter and
Arp designed backdrops and scenery. The poetry performances
became more and more extreme and abstract. 'Simultaneous
Poems', with titles such as 'The Admiral Seeks a House to Rent',
were interpreted by various voices at the same time to the accom-
paniment of whistles, bangs, groans, bells, drums and blows on
the table. Huelsenbeck would recite in German, Janco in English

# MOUVEMENT DADA

Manifeste, Vorträge, Kompositionen,
Tänze, Simultanische Dichtungen

Leitfaden durch die

## 8. DADA-SOIRÉE!

MITTWOCH, d. 9. April 1919
SAAL ZUR
## KAUFLEUTEN

*

**ANTIPHILOSOPHIE**

**I. Teil**

1. Viking Eggeling: Ueber abstrakte Kunst.
2. Suzanne Perrottet: Kompositionen von:
   a) Cyrill Scott Pavot
   b) Arnold Schönberg
   c) Erik Satie
3. Käthe Wulff: Gedichte von R. Hülsenbeck
   und W. Kandinsky.
4. Tristan Tzara: La fièvre du mâle
   (simultanistisches Gedicht
   unter Mitwirkung von 20
   Personen).

**II. Teil**

5. Hans Richter: Ueber Kunst und anderes.
6. Hans Heusser: Eigene Kompositionen:
   a) Vorspiel zu „Der weisse Berg"
   b) Drei Tanzrhythmen.
7. Hans Arp: Wolkenpumpe.
8. Suzanne Perrottet: Kompositionen von
   Arnold Schönberg.
9. Walter Serner: Manifest.

**III. Teil**

10. Noir Cacadou (Tanz, ausgeführt v. 5 Pers.
    unter Mitwirkung von Wulff)
11. Walter Serner: Eigene Gedichte
12. Tristan Tzara: Eigene Gedichte
    Proclamation Dada 1919
13. Hans Heusser: Eigene Kompositionen:
    a) Intime Harmonien
    b) Bergsage
    c) Klavier-Quartett in Es-dur

*

PREISE DER PLÄTZE:
Fr. 4.— und 2.—
Inventar bei KUONI und HUG.

**ZURICH**

Der Konzertflügel wurde
v d Firma P. Jecklin Söhne
zur Verfügung gestellt.

---

Soeben erschienen:

## DADA 4-5

Directeur: Tristan Tzara

MITARBEITER:

Louis Aragon, H. Arp, P. A. Birot, André
Breton, Gabrielle Buffet, G. Ribemont
Dessaigne, Viking Eggeling, Augusto Gia-
cometti, F, Hardekopf, R. Hausmann, Rich.
Huelsenbeck, M. Janco, W. Kandinsky, Paul
Klee, J. Perez-Jorba, Francis Picabia, R.
Radiguet, P. Reverdy, Mme. van Rees, H.
Richter, W. Serner, Ph. Soupault, Tr. Tzara

14 Illustrationen u. 2 Lithographien

Preis Fr. 2.50, Luxusausgabe Fr. 20.—

Demnächst erscheint:

## Das Hirngeschwür

Monatliche Publikation

Direktor: Walter Serner

Abonnement für 6 Nummern
10 Fr.

Vorbestellungen:

MOUVEMENT DADA
Zürich, Zeltweg 83.

---

## COLLECTION DADA

ZURICH
Zeltweg 83

and Tzara in French, each contrapuntally reciting against the other. The subject of the Simultaneous Poem, Hugo Ball tells us, was the essential quality of the human voice itself, '. . . the noises represent the inarticulate, inexorable and ultimately decisive forces which constitute the background. The poem carries the message that mankind is swallowed up in a mechanistic process.'

At the foot of the leaflet issued at the time of the performance of 'The Admiral Seeks a House to Rent', which contains the notated text of the poem, there is a section baldly headed 'Notes pour les Bourgeois', in which the background and development of the Simultaneous Poem is described. Stating that the poets wished to arrive at a transformation of their material similar to that of the Cubist painters, it points out that Villiers de l'Isle Adam had parallel intentions in the theatre, and that some years before Mallarmé had attempted typographical reform in his poems. Marinetti had earlier popularized a subordination of the text to its visual appearance, as had also Apollinaire, who by accentuating the central images typographically gave the 'possibility of beginning to read a poem from all sides at the same time'. Another French poet, Divoire, who preceded the Dadaists, was perhaps a little closer to the final Zürich results in that he sought a musical effect in 'orchestrating' the final poem.

Tzara, who signed the 'Notes pour les Bourgeois', states, however, that he would like to realize 'a poem based on other principles. Ones that provide the possibility that I should give to each listener the chance to link for himself suitable associations. It would hold the characteristic elements of his personality, intermingled, fragmented, etc., remaining nevertheless in the direction in which the author canalizes it.' This was a new aesthetic, a new concept of the poem, and was to develop, particularly after the founding of the magazine *Dada* in the following year, into a central point of Dada thinking, that the relationship between artist and spectator is an essential part of the work itself.

It is quite typical of the Dada spirit that no one knows when or how the word was invented or what it means; and there has characteristically been much mystification and wrangling between various claimants for the discovery of the term. Huelsenbeck maintains that it was discovered by Ball and himself by means of slipping a paper-knife in the pages of a dictionary

Poster for Dada soirée 1919

when they were looking for a stage name for a young singer in the cabaret. Richter, who arrived in Zürich after the word was already in circulation, remarks that he assumed that the derivation was from the Slavonic affirmative 'da, da' with which the Rumanians Tzara and Janco punctuated their violent and noisy conversations. Some years later, at a time when other claimants staked themselves as inventors, Hans Arp wrote characteristically in an issue of the magazine *Dada* dated 1921 that:

I hereby declare that Tristan Tzara found the word on 8 February 1916, at six o'clock in the afternoon: I was present with my twelve children when Tzara for the first time uttered this word which filled us with justified enthusiasm. This occurred at the Café de la Terasse in Zürich and I was wearing a brioche in my left nostril. I am convinced that this word is of no importance and that only imbeciles and Spanish professors can take an interest in dates. What interests us is the Dada spirit and we were all Dada before Dada came into existence . . .

In French the word means hobby-horse or rocking-horse, in German it denotes extreme naïveté or baby-talk, in some Italian dialects it means a dice, and the word exists elsewhere in other languages. But whatever its roots, or however it came to the light of day, it is finally a nonsense term that embodies the attitudes of Dada, attitudes which Gabrielle Buffet who became the wife of Picabia said were difficult to define, since 'Dada aspires to escape from everything that is common or ordinary or sensible. Dada does not recognize any tradition, any influence, or indeed any limits. Dada is a spontaneous product of life: a sort of cerebral mushroom which can appear and grow in every soil. Dada cannot be defined: it reveals itself.'

Dada was not essentially a historical period, but was, indeed still is, an emotional, social and political condition, a point of view. As far as a strict art-historical definition goes, it was a series of events in the arts covering painting, literature, theatre and music that took place more or less simultaneously in different places between 1912 and 1923. The two dates mark, at one extreme, events which occurred in Paris and New York that were completely in the spirit of Dada before the invention of the term and

*Nouvelle Série*

*Littérature* no. 3 1922 cover

were not necessarily known to the participants in Zürich, and, at the other extreme, the assimilation of the 'movement' into the more programmatic Surrealist Group whose advent André Breton proclaimed in 1924.

Breton, though later the 'Pope of Surrealism', its most profound thinker, and arguably the most important philosopher of art of our time, was himself active in Dada before he announced its demise. He was deeply aware of the universal nature of Dada, of the fact that it crossed the barriers of mere aesthetics. He wrote in an issue of his magazine *Littérature*:

Cubism was a school of painting, Futurism a political movement: Dada is a state of mind. To oppose one against the other reveals ignorance or bad faith. Free-thinking in religion does not resemble a church. Dada is artistic free-thinking. As long as they say prayers in the schools under the form of explanations of texts or trips through museums, we will cry out against despotism and attempt to disturb the ceremony. Dada devotes itself to nothing, neither to love nor to work. It is inadmissible that man should leave a trace of his passage on the earth. Dada, only recognizing instinct, condemns explanations *a priori*. According to Dada we can keep no control over ourselves. We must cease to think about these dogmas: morality and taste.

If Dada was a state of mind, though, it is important to recognize that it was a state conditioned by the social and historical conditions in which it existed; that, indeed, it was these conditions that gave it birth. Breton remarks that Futurism was a political movement, and so it was, in its later stages at least. Mussolini's personal involvement with the Futurist painters and his friendship with their leading theoretician, Marinetti, coloured the artistic movement and led it into Fascism. Dada, though never a coherent movement in the Futurist sense, since its central iconoclasm and irreverence prevented any sort of programme or ideology developing, had, however, a political nature.

The beginnings of Dada, Tzara has stated, 'were not the beginnings of art, but of disgust'. For the Dadaists, the 1914 war confirmed the total bankruptcy of nineteenth-century bourgeois society, a society presently engaged in tearing itself to pieces. With paradoxes embedded at the roots of social values, with, for instance, what was regarded as criminal behaviour in peacetime becoming patriotism in war-time, the logic of society and the reason of the bourgeois was seen as being manifestly illogical and unreasonable. As a result of this the Dadaists held the apparently irrational notion that the completely gratuitous and 'meaningless' act was the most reasonable. Breton had once described 'the most simple surrealist act' as 'going down the street ... and shooting at the crowd'. This inversion of conventional moral values, that in a society whose values were collapsing violence and aggression were as logical as accepted sociable attitudes, was implicit in Huelsenbeck's statement that he wished to make literature 'with a gun in hand', or in the flamboyant gestures of such Dada heroes as Arthur Cravan, who was in the habit of punctuating his lectures with random pistol shots.

During the summer of 1916 Leo Trotsky remarked that, 'One result of this war is that it has reduced art to bankruptcy.' If by that he meant, which one suspects he didn't, not only bourgeois art but also the emergent formal abstraction, the Dadaists would have agreed with him, for as Tzara suggested, the aim was to 'humiliate' art, to put it in a 'subordinate place in the supreme movement measured only in terms of life'. The moral and existential experience was considered to be superior to the merely aesthetic which entailed the values of a collapsing society. The intention of Dada, according to Hugo Ball, was '. . . a gladiatorial gesture . . . a public execution of false morality'.

The most obvious aspect of Dada, particularly in its early days, was a savage anarchism, a deliberate programme devised to undermine the moral and social assumptions of existing middle-class society. It is not so surprising that the group of wild young artists who created so much disturbance in Zürich should have also attracted attention from the local police. But it was a true Dada inconsequence that the same police should have ignored the quiet and well-behaved Russian gentleman who lived in a flat opposite the Café Voltaire: Vladimir Ilych Lenin, who not only plotted to, but actually succeeded in overturning the bourgeois world the Dadaists teased and taunted.

## Anti-art and the irrational

It is difficult in the Dada context of ambiguity and paradox to understand what was meant by the word 'art'. It is almost as if everybody held to their own private meaning, yet there was a certain consistency. 'All pictorial or plastic work is useless . . .' thundered Tzara in the manifesto of 1918; but Schwitters affirmed that '. . . everything the artist spits is art'. Disillusionment was the ultimate in nearly everything that Dada represented. Richter pointed out that art must be 'set on its way towards new functions which could only be known after the total negation of everything that had existed before. Until then: riot, destruction, defiance, confusion. The role of chance, not as an extension of the scope of art, but as a principle of dissolution and anarchy. In art, anti-art.'

Art was the symbol of bourgeois culture that was to be unrelentingly attacked, but at the same time, art was anything and everything. Art was both the petrified past, self-enclosed, set in an academic discipline, representing the culture that Marinetti so violently attacked, '. . . we wish to destroy the museums, the libraries, to fight against moralism, feminism and all opportunistic and utilitarian means', and at the same time it was the total, the existential experience of being in the world, as expressed by Huelsenbeck in the first German Dada manifesto of 1918: 'Art in its execution and direction is dependent on the time in which it lives, and artists are creatures of their epoch. The highest art will be that which in its conscious content presents the thousandfold problems of the day.'

Though today we can recognize certain stylistic qualities which immediately identify a particular painting as Dada, at the time the imagery of individual artists was diffuse and widespread. Some work such as that of Janco and Richter was clearly rooted in German Expressionism, others like Picabia and Duchamp demonstrated an interest in machine images, Geometric Abstraction appears in the work of Arp and Sophie Taeuber. One of the most curious of the minor figures at Zürich was Augusto Giacometti (the uncle of the sculptor), who painted in an informal abstract manner which pre-dated Tachism by over thirty years. The highly programmed formal abstractions of the Swedish artist Viking Eggeling are related to Constructivism and De Stijl, while both

Tatlin and Van Doesburg considered themselves briefly to be Dadaists, the latter even working under a Dada *nomme de plume* as I. K. Bonset, without deviating from their Constructivist styles.

With true Dada irony, flimsy, gratuitous or violent work, which was considered as 'anti-art', as, in Arp's words, '. . . art without sense . . . without meaning, as Nature is', has acquired with the passage of time an 'aesthetic' quality. A curious process seems to take place when an object is placed in a museum or gallery environment. The 'readymades' of Duchamp, originally objects of great ironic or shock value, can now be seen as extremely beautiful in the conventional sense of the balanced relationships of plastic and formal elements. Schwitters's collages of junk, rubbish and scraps of paper now seem to possess a sustained and intense lyricism unequalled by any other modern artist with the possible exception of Paul Klee.

Perhaps, without meaning to, the Dadaists did create 'art'. One wonders what would be the reactions of the more iconoclastic, had they survived, to seeing their paintings, sculptures and 'objects' enshrined in museums and regarded as historical examples of a cultural tradition. Indeed, did they turn over in their graves, roaring with ironical laughter, at the spectacle of the Zürich city dignitaries solemnly fixing, on 5 February 1966, the fiftieth anniversary of the opening night, a commemorative plaque to the building that had once been the Café Voltaire?

For Dada did contribute an aesthetic, extend our collective visual and perceptual experience, broaden our mental horizons. In the act of attempting to 'humiliate' art, through the idea of the *Gesamtkunstwerk*, the 'total work of art', the beginnings of what we would now call 'multi-media art', inherited from Kandinsky, the ordinary and everyday was imbued with aesthetic significance.

It is more specifically in the techniques that the Dadaists used, and the philosophical implication inherent in these techniques, that Dada produced its unique contribution; a contribution that can be seen as not so much merely adding to a tradition, as shifting the whole mainstream, as it were, into a new river-bed.

*Dadaco* 1920 trial sheet

# DADA

Was ist **dada**?

Eine Kunst? Eine Philosophie? eine Politik?

**Eine Feuerversicherung?**

Oder: *Staatsreligion?*

ist **dada** wirkliche ENERGIE?

oder ist es ▬ **Garnichts**, d. h.

alles?

Die Geister einer unbedeutenden Epoche sind vor eine große und schwere Aufgabe gestellt. Wo die Wirklichkeit, zu der alles Geistige in engster Beziehung steht und von der es den stärksten Teil seiner Antriebe erhält, in höchsten Taumel gerissen ist, wo ein Tag verneint, was der vorhergehende heiligte, wo die Ereignisse sich überstürzen wie

DONNERSCHLÄGE

ist es schwerer als in ruhiger Zeit, das Maaß der Persönlichkeit auszubalancieren und den Kreis zu formieren, aus dem man als gesammelte Erscheinung aufwächst. Es fehlt das, was man die Schule der Geistigkeit nennen kann. Derjenige, der im Ausdruck seiner Gedanken seine Lebensarbeit sieht, bleibt am Anfang der Entwicklung auf das Wort und die Tat der Vorhergehenden angewiesen. Unwillkürlich richten sich die Augen des jungen Dichters auf die ältere Generation; je weniger sicher er sich fühlt, umsomehr ist er bestrebt, aus dem Leben der Väter ein Ziel zu suchen, das ihm für ein gemeinsames Streben verbindlich zu sein scheint. Die Tradition ist ein mächtiges Agens, das in den bedeutendsten Kulturen immer wieder gesucht und hervorgehoben wird. Die französische Geistigkeit ist ohne die Tradition nicht denkbar und immer wieder steht jemand auf, der das Genie latein preist, wie es sich von Rabelais bis Anatol France, bestimmt von klimatischen und völkischen Verhältnissen geäußert hat. Immer wieder hat es dort eine Renaissance francaise gegeben und mit dem Eigentümlichen des französischen Geistes wie es von Vätern und Großvätern gehandhabt worden ist, wäre die Kultur des Landes dahin. Dies Gemeinsame, dies Abstrakte hinter der Fülle der einzelnen Erscheinungen hat die Jugend von jeher gesucht, um sich eine Schule daraus zu machen. Es ist der Sinn für Verehrung und Begeisterung, eine Eigenschaft der Zwanzigjährigen, die sie dazu befähigt, sie sucht Gemeinschaft, Freundschaftsbünde, Klubs, in denen man Alles diskutieren kann, um das Neue daraus wachsen zu lassen. Dies natürliche Bedürfnis bildete die Handwerks- und Malschulen, aus der die große Kunst des Mittelalters hervorging. Die Jugend allein hat das Recht und das Vorrecht, sich unter zu ordnen, weil sie allein aus einem Abhängigkeitsverhältnis gestärkt hervorgehen kann, weil sie allein eine Bildung des Charakters findet, wo andere in Knechtschaft und Infamie herabsinken. Aber wo findet die Jugend einer Epoche wie die unsere, die Möglichkeit sich Lehrer zu suchen, von deren Lippen sie Klugheit und Weltweisheit kennen lernen kann, in deren Büchern sie den

**Tretet Dada bei**

DIW Küße siƨen auff den TELE grap hen sTangen

SINN DER wELT

suchen und finden könnte?

**Augusto Giacometti** *Colour Abstraction* about 1913 pastel cut-out
mounted on paper $10\frac{1}{4} \times 9\frac{5}{8}$ in.
Museum of Modern Art, New York, gift of Ernst Beyeler

**Augusto Giacometti** *Summer Night* 1917 oil on canvas 26½ × 25⅝ in.
Museum of Modern Art, New York

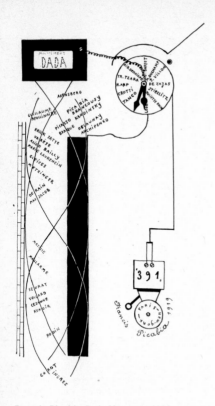

**Francis Picabia** *Dada Movement* 1919 pen and ink $20\frac{1}{8} \times 14\frac{1}{4}$ in.
Museum of Modern Art, New York

One family of images that is dominant in Dada painting, as in
the abstract sound poetry of Huelsenbeck, Tzara and Schwitters,
is concerned with machinery.

The social upheavals at the beginning of the century, indeed
those that we are still currently enduring, are inseparable from the
environment in which they took place. The technological society
that began with the industrial revolution, and which has during
recent years developed apace with the second electronic and
cybernetic revolution, was round about 1908 at a crucial point
in its history. It was during that year that Cubism appeared,

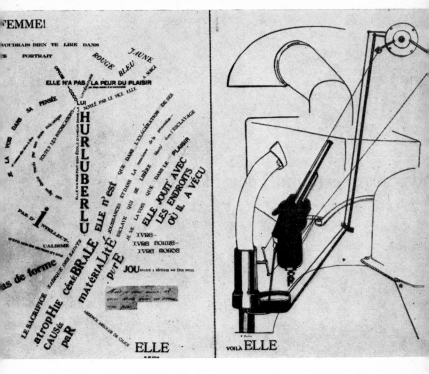

From *291* 1915
*Left* Marius de Zayas *Elle: Right* Francis Picabia *Voilà Elle*

paralleled by Schönberg's development of atonal music, by the 'fragmentation' of the novel's previously linear form, and by the psychoanalytic thinking of Freud and Jung. About the same time Max Planck published his *Quantum Theory*, Einstein *Relativity*, and the existential philospher Husserl his *Logical Investigations*. And a new set of assumptions about the nature of the universe took on a tangible form in the appearance of the motor-car, the assembly-line factory, the aeroplane, the wireless and the gramophone. The technological society and the mechanical world to which we are still attempting to adjust came to birth in

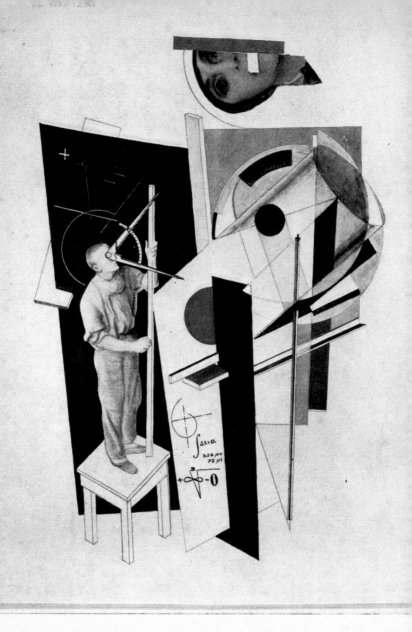

**El Lissitzky** *Tatlin Working on the Third International Sculpture* about 1920
collage 13 × 9½ in. Grosvenor Gallery, London

**Hans Arp** *Automatic Drawing* 1916 brush and ink on brownish paper
16¾ × 21¼ in. Museum of Modern Art, New York

the first ten years of this century, totally altering the nature of our
environment; and the artist reacted to this cultural shift. In
philosophy, the emergent ideas that came to be known as
Phenomenology and Existentialism showed a new network of
relationships in the universe, and psychology, particularly that of
Freud, revealed the unconscious, the world of irrationality that
exists deep within each of us. The Dadaists were concerned with
the irrational in their ideas of the gratuitous gesture, but also the
irrational was made use of in terms of direct techniques of painting: and it is here that we find their most significant contribution
to the visual arts, for it led directly to Surrealism, and by extension
to Abstract Expressionism, Action Painting, Parisian Tachism and
Pop Art. Without the Dadaists the flavour and content of the
visual arts today would have been fundamentally different.

**Hans Arp** *Collage with Squares Arranged according to the Laws of Chance* 1916–17 collage of coloured papers 19⅛ × 13⅝ in. Museum of Modern Art, New York

**Hans Arp** *Birds in an Aquarium* about 1920 painted wood relief 9⅞ × 8 in. Museum of Modern Art, New York

When a Dadaist spoke of the desire for a total freedom, it was not merely the deadweight of nineteenth-century middle-class culture that he was opposing, nor was he thinking mainly in political terms. The freedom sought was also that from rationality itself, from logic and from order, from the familiar and the accepted. 'The absence of any ulterior motive,' writes Hans Richter,

**Hans Arp** from 'Arpaden', a portfolio of 7 reproductions of drawings about 1918 each 17¾ × 13¾ in. Museum of Modern Art, New York

a *The Navel Bottle*   b *Eggbeater*   c *Moustache Hat*   d *Moustache Watch*

**Hans Arp** *Deux Petits sous un Arbre* 1931 $25\frac{1}{2}$ × $18\frac{1}{8}$ × $18\frac{1}{8}$ in.
Galerie A.-F.Petit, Paris

enables us to listen to the voice of the "Unknown"—and to draw knowledge from the realm of the unknown.' And it was discovered that this 'unknown', a power-source of imagery and symbolism, was released by the technical use of the gesture, of the chance configuration.

A seminal point in the development of Dada, at least as far as the fine arts are concerned, was provided by the painter Hans Arp, who, working one day on a drawing that was conventional though abstract, found that he was not managing to get the image to work, to get the drawing to coalesce in the manner that he wanted it to. In exasperation he tore it up and threw the pieces on the ground, to be immediately struck by the fact that the random pattern in which the scraps of paper had fallen exactly expressed the particular quality he had earlier been attempting to achieve. From that time he experimented with aleatory factors, shuffling cut-out pieces of coloured paper on sheets of cardboard, and

**Max Ernst** a *frottage* from *Histoire naturelle* 1926
Galerie Jeanne Bucher, Paris

gumming the elements down in the chance relationships they made one with the other.

This discovery of the irrational was to be one of the central concepts of the Dada 'aesthetic', if one can use that word. It was exploited in the 'automatic' writing of poems by literally pulling

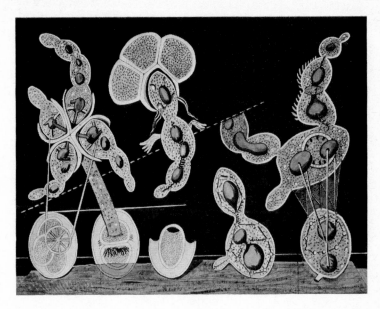

**Max Ernst** *The Gramineous Bicycle Garnished with Bells* 1920 anatomical chart altered with gouache 29¼ × 39¼ in.
Museum of Modern Art, New York

words out of a hat; it was to be exploited, particularly by the Berlin group, by the collaging together of photographic images; it was to be exploited by Max Ernst with two techniques he is credited with inventing, or at least making specifically his own, those of *frottage* and *decalcomania*, the production of images in

**Max Ernst** a *frottage* from *Histoire naturelle* 1926
Galerie A.-F. Petit, Paris

the first case by rubbing a chalk or some other medium across a
rough or textured surface, in the second by blotting images on to
paper from wet paint.

From the random forms that Ernst produced he read and isolated images that his conscious mind was too inhibited or pre-
conditioned to discover. Leonardo, of course, long ago, sought
battles, disasters, cities and great floods in the stains on a plaster
wall. With the Rorschach blot, the trained psychoanalyst can
coax previously unrecognized obsessions and fantasies from his
patient's mind. The Dadaists, for their part, explored and exploited
the irrational, an unconditioned landscape of images in which they
saw not only artistic and creative freedom but also the complete
existential freedom of man shackled in a society whose concepts
and assumptions appeared to be totally arbitrary and meaningless.

## The roots of Dada

The statements of the Café Voltaire circle make clear the anti-militarist, libertarian, not to say directly anarchist and utopian, attitudes of Zürich Dada. The political climate of Europe (and the political climate conditions and shapes the aesthetic) had been developing upon lines leading inevitably towards Dada for half a century. The Romantic movement in the arts, for example, dominating the years prior to the half-way mark of the nineteenth century, was inextricably linked with the emergent industrial revolution, with the altered environment conditioned by machinery. This new social environment was responsible for producing not only the Communist Manifesto of 1846 and all its implications but also engendered a radically new attitude in the world of artists and intellectuals: it was responsible for the appearance of the 'bohemian'.

In reaction to the rationalism of the eighteenth century the artist progressively moved into the stance of the outsider, and High Romantics such as Blake and Byron actively challenged the *status quo*. By the mid-nineteenth century the artist, who previously had been a solitary and professional man, was banding together with his fellows, developing not merely an aesthetic but also a common ideological anti-bourgeois platform. The epoch of schools and isms had come about, the individual artist had begun to assume the role of *saboteur* and social terrorist. With this new group identity, firmly opposed to the established mores, he created a sub-culture; art came 'out into life', the gesture or the act began to assume a parallel importance with the work, the deed to complement the idea.

The development of bohemia and that of the Black International were parallel, contemporary and interrelated. Society during the first few years of the 1890s was outraged by a series of anarchist bomb attacks; the 'propaganda of the deed' as perpetrated by Ravachol, Vaillant and Emile Henri, led the extremist political commentator Laurent Tailhade to remark '. . . what do a few human lives matter *si le geste est beau?*', a statement which would be echoed in the ironic nihilism of the bohemians. It was also a statement which stands as a prototype of later Futurist or Dada pronouncements, and it is worth noting that Tailhade fell himself to the supreme irony of chance, being severely injured in a later terrorist *geste*, when a crowded restaurant in which he was quietly having dinner was bombed.

By the end of the century the beginnings of anti-art and the first explorations of chance were well under way. Rimbaud's hallucinatory vision charted the innocent eye; not to mention his experimenting with the synaesthesia that was to become so important to the Dadaists, when he apportioned different colours to each vowel. Lautréamont captured the climate of the irrational in his extraordinary book *The Song of Maldoror,* Huysmans

*Opposite*
**Marcel Duchamp** *Bicycle Wheel* 1913 readymade (replica)
Collection Richard Hamilton, London

**Giacomo Balla** *The Violinist* 1912 oil on canvas 20½ × 29½ in.
Collection Eric Estorick, London

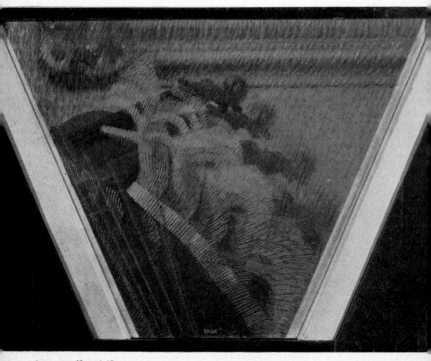

*On pages 42 and 43*
Duchamp in his studio

celebrated not only the gratuitous action but also the abstract beauty of the locomotive, and the nonsense verses of Edward Lear and Christian Morgenstern, the fantasies of Lewis Carroll, penetrated, like Rousseau's paintings, into hitherto unmapped areas of primitivism.

But if anyone can be called the father of Dadaism, it surely must be Alfred Jarry, who with his monstrous creation of Ubu Roi symbolized and castigated the bourgeoisie of the late nineteenth century. Ubu was originally created as a lampoon upon a teacher while Jarry was still at school, and he haunted the author until his death in 1907. Jarry also 'invented', through the person of his character Dr Faustroll, the science of Pataphysics, the ironic 'science of imaginary solutions', in which the admirable Doctor maintains that the world consists of nothing but exceptions, and that the 'rule' is precisely an exception to an exception; while as far as the universe is concerned, Faustroll defined it as 'the exception to oneself'.

Jarry's novel *Le Surmâle*, published in 1902, emphasizes the influence of the machine in contemporary life. While Ubu and Faustroll are prophetic of the coming spirit of Dada, the Supermale is prophetic of one aspect of its future content. And it is this aspect which the Futurists picked up seven years later. The 'First Futurist Manifesto', signed by Marinetti, was printed in the Paris newspaper *Figaro* on 20 February 1909, and it stated that:

. . . we declare that the world's splendour has been enriched by a new beauty; the beauty of speed. A racing motor-car, its frame adorned with great pipes like snakes that have explosive breath— a roaring motor-car which looks as though it was running on shrapnel, is more beautiful than the *Victory of Samothrace* . . . we stand upon the extreme promontory of our culture!—Why should we look behind us when we have to break in the mysterious portals of the Impossible? Time and Space died yesterday. Already we live in the absolute, since we have already created speed, eternal and ever-present.

The machine, dynamism, speed and movement were the central premises of the Futurist idea. Not only did they wish to break with the static museum art of the past, but with any fixed location at all. Movement implies multiplicity, '. . . the simultaneousness of states of mind in the work of art, that is the intoxicating aim of our

**Hans Arp** *Forest* 1916 painted wood relief $12\frac{5}{8} \times 8\frac{1}{4}$ in. Collection Sir Roland Penrose, London

art.' Where the Cubists saw the *static* object from a multiplicity of viewpoints, the Futurists observed it dynamically and simultaneously in diverse points of space *and* time. Balla, Boccioni, Carrà and Severini as painters explored this concept of 'simultaneity', while Luigi Russolo applied the same premises to music, collaging together in his 'art of noise' sounds from diverse extra-musical sources, breaking down the linear sequence of musical form and incorporating random and accidental effects.

In May 1912 Marinetti published 'The Technical Manifesto of Futurist Literature', in which, wishing to bring to bear some of the new attitudes discovered by painting, he declared that syntax must be broken down, that the old grammatical preconceptions of the roles of nouns, verbs, adjectives and conjunctions were no longer valid. He wished to replace conventional punctuation with mathematical signs like those which normally indicate equality, plus, minus or division. Working from a principle of analogy, he stated that '. . . after free-verse, here is *words in freedom*'.

This idea of 'words in freedom' was to become central to Dada activity, and is at the root of audio-visual concepts in the fine arts today. The conventional poem read off the page is an 'event' which occurs by and large in the reader's head. The poem constructed upon the principle of *words in freedom* is read aloud as a pure, non-figurative, auditory experience; at the same time, by the use of a characteristic and scored typography, it presents a visual parallel to the sound experience.

Marinetti's new abstract poetry was to influence the young poets of Paris, paralleling and developing the already existing influence of Apollinaire, while at the same time a large exhibition of Futurist paintings at the Galerie Bertheim Jeune in 1911 doubtless affected such artists as Léger, Delaunay, Picabia and Duchamp. The same exhibition travelled the following year to London, where it was well received by the Futurist-inspired Vorticist group, a collection of English artists including Bomberg and Nevilson and led by Wyndham Lewis, whose magazine *Blast* owed much in its layout to 'words in freedom'. As a result of the activities of the English artists, the Vorticist version of the modern spirit took a strong, though brief, hold in London, though,

Strepito  ferraglie                    Bran-
colamenti   ubbriaco.          **SALITA**
                                              locomotiva

4000    gradi    febbre    asmatica
                    Vene    ferro    barometro    vapo-

re - mercurio          *SALIRE*
          *SALIRE  SALIRE*
                              Volute    fumo
propaggini   cielo

# CIELO  CIELO  CIELO

acqua   saponata   bacinella   roveseiata   di   postribolo

## GALLERIA   ventre   di   bale-

na                    Trasudazione                    Ter-
mometro   mie   vene   pneumatiche   inturgidirsi

# LUCE  ARIA  MAREORAMA

mio   cervello   barnum   immagini   Sole   balenio   cascate
miglio
        TRABALLAMENTI     BECCHEGGIO
                    RULLIO
Intonazione   musica   ferraglie   sirena   locomotiva'
                fiiiiischi
fischi                                    fiiiiischi
        fiischi            fiiiiischi

**LUIGI RUSSOLO**   accordare   prodigio   suoi
STRADIVARI   FUTURISTI.

*Armando Mazza*
**futurista**

perhaps because of the physical isolation and comparative social stability of England, it never developed on Dada lines as elsewhere.

In 1912, however, it looked as if London might provide the exact climate required for the Futurist experiment. Industrialization was there more advanced than anywhere else in Europe, and Marinetti was himself very much taken by the British music hall, calling it the 'theatre of surprises', and stating that it was '. . . the only theatre which makes use of the collaboration of the public'. In the summer of 1914 Marinetti published a joint manifesto with the English painter Nevilson, and arranged a week of concerts at the London Coliseum, which performances were a great success in *avant-garde* terms, bewildering and provoking a hostile audience. But within a few months, the sudden outbreak of hostilities brought the Futurist movement to an abrupt end everywhere except in the land of its origin, where it continued and developed in isolation until the 1930s, and took on certain Fascist characteristics during the second half of its lifetime. Some aspects of Futurism, however, particularly the attitude towards machinery, much influenced at an early date two young Paris-based painters, both of whom were to escape the war by travelling to America. Duchamp and Picabia were to provide the link between Futurism and the imminent Dada explosion.

# New York—Duchamp and philosophical irony

One of the most extraordinary, certainly one of the most influential art events in the modern movement was the exhibition that has gone down in history as the 'Armory Show'. This took place in New York in February 1913. Its real title was the 'International Exhibition of Modern Art' and it was mounted in a large building not normally used for art exhibitions, the armoury of the 69th Infantry Regiment on Lexington Avenue.

Though he was not directly associated with the Armory Show itself, it was a photographer, Alfred Stieglitz, whose activities during the preceding years prepared the ground for the astonishing impact this exhibition was to have, and he subsequently was the pivot of pre-Dada and Dada activities in America. Stieglitz, one of the pioneers of modern photography, together with his friend Edward Steichen, founded in 1902 the 'Photo-Secession', an association of modern photographers. A few years later he opened a gallery at 291 Fifth Avenue, which, though originally proposing exhibitions of photography, soon began to show the new painting emanating from Paris.

The gallery, which was first called 'Camera Work', but later changed its name to '291' was without question the centre of artistic activity in New York at that time and it was largely responsible for the developing shift in the artistic climate which reached a climax at the Armory exhibition. The 'sensation' of that show was not a work by Picasso or any of the other Cubists, but the now famous painting by Duchamp, *Nude Descending a Staircase.* Overnight it was a *succès de scandale*. The painting was attacked and made fun of, one newspaper commentator describing it with the succinct and memorable phrase by which he earned a small slot in art history, as an 'explosion in a shingle factory'.

The work that Duchamp was engaged in around 1912 in Paris had a very distinctive flavour and character, though it could be said to have developed more or less from Cubist premises. The Cubists themselves considered Duchamp to have defected to the Futurists, and on one famous occasion asked him to withdraw his *Nude* from the Salon des Indépendants at which the 'reasonable' Cubists were showing. Duchamp had, in fact, never seen a Futurist picture when he painted his *Nude* and preceding studies, the first Futurist show in Paris not having taken place until

**Marcel Duchamp** *Nude Descending a Staircase* 1912 oil on canvas 58 × 35 in.
Philadelphia Museum of Art, Louise and Walter Arensberg Collection

**Marcel Duchamp** *The Passage from the Virgin to the Bride* 1912 oil on canvas
$23\frac{3}{8} \times 21\frac{1}{4}$ in.
Museum of Modern Art, New York

February 1912. However, there would seem to be a common source of imagery; both painters such as Balla or Severini and Duchamp were fascinated by the study of movement and time in the stop-action and composite photographs of Etienne Marey, which were being widely reproduced in popular journals at the time.

Despite a common interest in sequence and movement, Duchamp nevertheless was taking up a position as distinct from the Futurists as from the Cubists. He was, in fact, rebelling against what he called 'retinal painting'. 'I was interested,' he has stated, 'in ideas, not merely in visual products . . . I wanted to put

**Marcel Duchamp** *King and Queen Surrounded by Swift Nudes* 1912 oil on canvas 45½ × 50¾ in.
Philadelphia Museum of Art, Louise and Walter Arensberg Collection

# APOLINÈRE ENAMELED

[from] MARCEL DUCHAMP 1916 1917

Marcel Duchamp *Girl with Bedstead (Apolinère Enameled)* 1916–17 readymade 9¼ × 13¼ in. long.
Philadelphia Museum of Art, Louise and Walter Arensberg Collection

painting once again at the service of the mind.' The *Nude* was not yet a Dada work, least of all in terms of style, but certain attitudes that lay behind its conception contained the germs of Dada. The picture itself, was, as the painter called it, '... a static representation of movement'; but it was not abstract, for as Duchamp took care to emphasize, his aim was a process of *reduction* rather than one of *abstraction*. 'Reduce, reduce, reduce was my thought. But at the same time *my aim was turning inward* ... I came to feel that an artist might use anything—a dot, a line, the most conventional or unconventional symbol—to say what he wanted to say ... for all this reduction I would never call it abstract painting.'

The desire to put 'painting once again at the service of the mind' is the key to the work of Duchamp. He is said to have invented the word 'cervelle', meaning 'brain-fact', to describe a fundamental content of his work, particularly the Readymades, the manufactured objects which he maintained became works of art by virtue of his simply saying that they were, of his act of choosing the object, elevating and isolating it.

APROPOS OF ' READYMADES '

IN 1913 I HAD THE HAPPY IDEA TO FASTEN A BICYCLE WHEEL TO A KITCHEN STOOL AND WATCH IT TURN.

A FEW MONTHS LATER I BOUGHT A CHEAP REPRODUCTION OF A WINTER EVENING LANDSCAPE, WHICH I CALLED ' PHARMACY ' AFTER ADDING TWO SMALL DOTS , ONE RED AND ONE YELLOW, IN THE HORIZON.

IN NEW YORK IN 1915 I BOUGHT AT A HARDWARE STORE A SNOW SHOVEL, ON WHICH I WROTE ' IN ADVANCE OF THE BROKEN ARM '.

It WAS AROUND THAT TIME that THE WORD ' READYMADE ' CAME TO MY MIND TO DESIGNATE THIS FORM OF MANIFESTATION.

A POINT WHICH I VERY MUCH WANT TO ESTABLISH IS THAT THE CHOICE OF THESE ' READYMADES ' WAS NEVER DICTATED BY AN ESTHETIC DELECTATION.

THIS CHOICE WAS BASED ON A REACTION OF VISUAL INDIFFERENCE WITH AT THE SAME TIME A TOTAL ABSENCE OF GOOD OR BAD TASTE.... IN FACT A COMPLETE ANESTHESIA.

ONE IMPORTANT CHARACTERISTIC WAS THE SHORT SENTENCE WHICH I OCCASIONALLY INSCRIBED ON THE ' READYMADE '.

THAT SENTENCE INSTEAD OF DESCRIBING THE OBJECT LIKE A TITLE WAS MEANT TO CARRY THE MIND OF THE SPECTATOR TOWARDS OTHER REGIONS MORE VERBAL.

SOMETIMES I WOULD ADD A GRAPHIC DETAIL OF PRESENTATION WHICH IN ORDER TO SATISFY MY CRAVING FOR ALLITERATIONS, WOULD BE CALLED ' READYMADE AIDED '.

AT ANOTHER TIME WANTING TO EXPOSE THE BASIC ANTINOMY BETWEEN ART AND READYMADES I IMAGINED A ' RECIPROCAL READYMADE ' , USE A REMBRANDT AS AN IRONING BOARD !.

I REALIZED VERY SOON THE DANGER OF REPEATING INDISCRIMINATELY THIS FORM OF EXPRESSION AND DECIDED TO LIMIT THE PRODUCTION OF ' READYMADES ' TO A SMALL NUMBER YEARLY. I WAS AWARE AT THAT TIME , THAT FOR THE SPECTATOR EVEN MORE THAN FOR THE ARTIST, ART IS A HABIT FORMING DRUG AND I WANTED TO PROTECT MY ' READYMADES ' AGAINST SUCH A CONTAMINATION.

ANOTHER ASPECT OF THE ' READYMADE ' IS ITS LACK OF UNIQUENESS... THE REPLICA OF A ' READYMADE ' DELIVERING THE SAME MESSAGE, IN FACT NEARLY EVERY ONE OF THE existing today ' READYMADES ' IS NOT AN ORIGINAL IN THE CONVENTIONAL SENSE.

A FINAL REMARK TO THIS EGOMANIAC'S DISCOURSE :

SINCE THE TUBES OF PAINT USED BY THE ARTIST ARE MANUFACTURED AND READY MADE PRODUCTS WE MUST CONCLUDE THAT ALL THE PAINTINGS IN THE WORLD ARE ' READYMADES AIDED ' AND ALSO WORKS OF ASSEMBLAGE.

marcel duchamp '61

**Marcel Duchamp** *In Advance of the Broken Arm* 1945 readymade 47¾ in. high
Yale University Art Gallery, gift of Katherine S. Dreiser

"In 1913 I had the happy idea to fasten a bicycle wheel to a kitchen stool and watch it turn.

A few months later I bought a cheap reproduction of a winter evening landscape, which I called 'Pharmacy' after adding two small dots, one red and one yellow, in the horizon.

In New York in 1915 I bought at a hardware store a snow shovel on which I wrote 'In advance of the broken arm'.

It was around that time that the word 'readymade' came to my mind to designate this form of manifestation.

A point that I want very much to establish is that the choice of these 'readymades' was never dictated by aesthetic delectation.

The choice was based on a reaction of *visual* indifference with at the same time a total absence of good or bad taste . . . in fact a complete anaesthesia.

One important characteristic was the short sentence which I occasionally inscribed on the 'readymade'.

That sentence instead of describing the object like a title was meant to carry the mind of the spectator towards other regions more verbal.

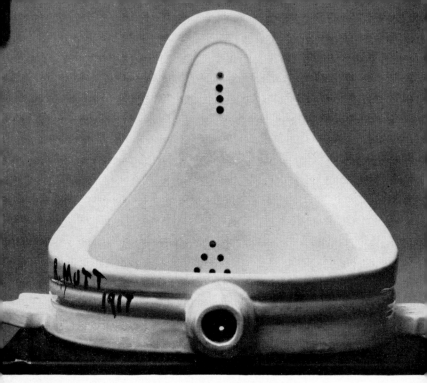

**Marcel Duchamp** *Fountain* 1917 readymade (replica) 24⅝ in. high
Galleria Schwarz, Milan

**Marcel Duchamp** *Self-portrait* 1959 serigraph 7⅞ × 7⅞ in.
Museum of Modern Art, New York, gift of Lang Charities Inc.

Sometimes I would add a graphic detail of presentation which, in order to satisfy my craving for alliterations, would be called 'readymade aided'.

At another time, wanting to expose the basic antinomy between art and 'readymades', I imagined a *'reciprocal readymade'* : use a Rembrandt as an ironing board !

I realized very soon the danger of repeating indiscriminately this form of expression and decided to limit the production of 'readymades' to a small number yearly. I was aware at that time, that for the spectator even more than for the artist, *art is a habit forming drug* and I wanted to protect my 'readymades' against such a *contamination*.

Another aspect of the 'readymade' is its lack of uniqueness . . . the replica of the 'readymade' delivering the same message, in fact nearly every one of the 'readymades' existing today is not an original in the conventional sense.

A final remark to this egomaniac's discourse :

Since the tubes of paint used by an artist are manufactured and

marcel Duchamp Le Havre 1959     marcel duchamp
3/60

**Marcel Duchamp** *Valise* 1942 containing 68 reproductions of works of Duchamp 15½ × 13¾ in.
Philadelphia Museum of Art, Louise and Walter Arensberg Collection

readymade products we must conclude that all the paintings in the world are 'readymades aided' and also works of assemblage.''

The readymade, as Duchamp has stressed, is not a work of art, but neither is it a work of anti-art, for the opposition of art must make use of analogous points of reference, must also be based on the process of aesthetic and sensory perception. But the ready-made is based upon 'visual indifference . . . complete anaesthesia'. The process is cerebral; the artist here is not making use of his instincts or his visual sensibility, but of a severe and rigorous rationality. He has applied the scientific method, used measurement and logic towards the discovery of a plastic vision, and more than any other artist, Duchamp has manipulated the language of technology to come to terms with a society based upon technology. Unlike many Dadaists, he was not satisfied with the merely iconoclastic or anarchic gesture, not satisfied with escaping from logic into the symbolic world of the irrational. Beyond the logic that he destroyed he erected a further logic, a self-consistent system that obeyed the *rationality* of his vision.

The bearded Mona Lisa, labelled L.H.O.O.Q., which letters pronounced phonetically in the French manner make up the phrase *Elle a chaud au cul,* savagely ridicules a cultural as well as an artistic totem, it also demolishes ingrained attitudes and allows an approach to 'art' unfettered with the concepts of the past.

This new approach is nowhere more evident, or more realized, than in Duchamp's major work, *The Bride Stripped Bare by her Bachelors, Even,* commonly called the *Large Glass.* This enormous work, constructed from a diversity of material including oil-paint, lead sheetings, wire foil, dust and varnish on two separate sheets of glass, took him eight years to complete. The actual work on the *Glass* spanned the years 1915 to 1923, though he had begun to think about the work some years before. In the late summer of 1912 he was already groping towards a radically new 'language' of art that would consist of graphic forms and literary allusions, but would inherently obey a whole structure of logic that was yet to be invented. By the end of 1914 he had assembled an enormous quantity of notes couched in mechanical and scientific terms that were particularly the artist's own.

It was almost as if he had to discover for himself a new mathematics, and elements of this were tried out in several paintings and small 'glasses'. For instance, with complete logic, and taking the principle of chance much further than Hans Arp with his torn paper, Duchamp 'invented' his own standard of measurement. The official metre, represented by a bar of platinum of a specific length related fractionally to the earth's circumference, and kept under controlled conditions of temperature and humidity in a Paris vault, seemed to the Dada mind no less arbitrary than any gratuitous scale of measurement. Duchamp, therefore, found his own scale; dropping three pieces of thread, each a metre in length, from an exact height of one metre, and carefully recording the resultant forms. These he christened the *Three Standard Stops.* On the model of the threads which, as he noted, had 'While

Marcel Duchamp *Chocolate Grinder* 1913 oil on canvas 24¾ × 25⅝ in. Philadelphia Museum of Art, Louise and Walter Arensberg Collection

*Opposite*
**Marcel Duchamp** *The Large Glass* or *The Bride Stripped Bare by her Bachelors, Even* 1915–23 oil and lead wire on glass 109¼ × 69⅛ in. Philadelphia Museum of Art

twisting at will [given] a new form to the unit of length', he made three wooden 'rulers' from draughtsman's straight-edges, and used these as basic structural elements in the *Large Glass.*

Together with the *Draught Pistons,* images arrived at by photographing a piece of netting moving randomly in a draught, and the *Shots,* which are nine holes drilled in the glass at positions determined by shooting at the glass with matchsticks dipped in paint and discharged from a toy cannon, the *Stops* make up the main chance-controlled deformations of the work. The random

**Francis Picabia** / *See Again in Memory My Dear Udnie* 1913 oil on canvas
98½ × 78¼ in. Museum of Modern Art, New York, Hillman Periodicals Fund

*Opposite*
**Marcel Duchamp** *Given, the Waterfall, the Gas Lamp* 1946–66 detail of
façade, mixed media assemblage
Philadelphia Museum of Art, gift of the Cassandra Foundation

element was also partially used during the process that became
known as the 'dust breeding'. The *Glass* was left alone for some
time and permitted to accumulate a layer of dust, which was at
one stage photographed by Man Ray, then gummed down in
specific areas with varnish, creating the *Seven Sieves*, the series
of cone-shaped forms in the lower half of the picture.

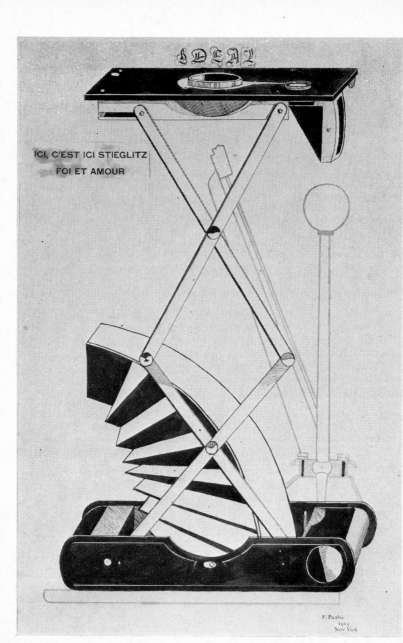

ICI, C'EST ICI STIEGLITZ
FOI ET AMOUR

IDEAL

F. Picabia
1915
New York

The actual images of the *Large Glass* are developments of an iconography which appeared in earlier works: the *Chocolate Grinder*, the *Water Mill*, the *Nine Malic Moulds* coalesce together to form the two fantastic and extraordinary 'machines'—the *Bride* on the upper panel, and the *Bachelors* on the lower. But in this work he has completed the transformation from the 'artist' of the very early works in, first a Fauve, then a Cubo-Futurist manner, via the 'anti-artist', to ultimately the 'engineer'. With the

**Francis Picabia** *Ici, c'est ici Stieglitz* 1915 pen and red and black ink 29⅞ × 20 in. Metropolitan Museum of Art, New York, Alfred Stieglitz Collection

**Francis Picabia** *Le Monde* 1919 pen and Indian ink 12½ × 9½ in. Hanover Gallery, London

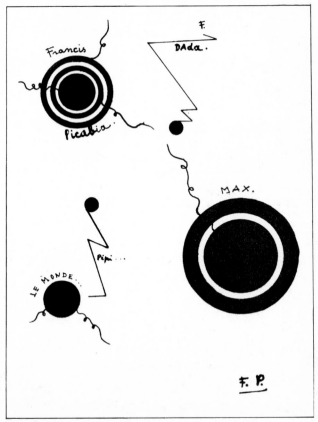

F. Picabia
19

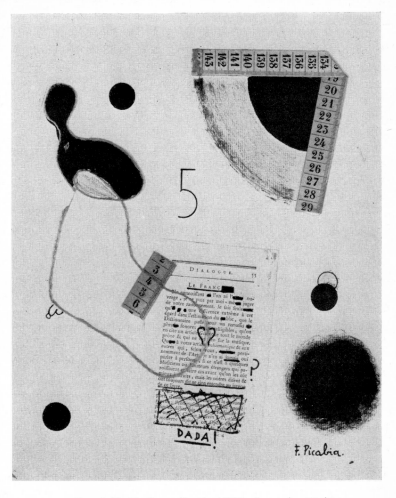

**Francis Picabia** *Composition* about 1919 collage and watercolour
$14\frac{1}{4} \times 11\frac{3}{4}$ in.
Hanover Gallery, London

*Opposite*
**Francis Picabia** *Mechanical Composition* 1919 watercolour 30 × 22 in.
Collection Mr and Mrs Lester Avnet, New York

*Large Glass,* art has become transmuted from an intuitive expressionist process to one that is very like that of the scientist, the process of research.

Picabia is a name frequently linked with that of Duchamp: the two artists were close friends and colleagues, and the Spanish painter's ebullient imagination combined with the Frenchman's logical irony made a formidable tandem. Picabia was himself connected with Stieglitz before the Armory show (the photographer gave him a one-man exhibition in 1913), but he did not move away from conventional Cubism, or rather Cubism of the type defined by Apollinaire as 'Orphism', until after that date. The impact of American technology, of architecture, bridges and machinery totally shifted his perspective, anticipating Duchamp's later statement that the best art that the country had produced was its plumbing and its bridges.

Working in a 'machine' style, Picabia was, however, fundamentally an ironist and a fantasist. Faced with objects, he attempted not merely to wrench them out of context, but to totally de-nature them. As early as 1915 he published in Stieglitz's magazine *291* a series of drawings which he called 'object portraits'. Stieglitz himself was represented by a camera, the 'typical American girl' by a sparking-plug, and a self-portrait was conceived in terms of a motor-car horn. All of these drawings were executed with the blandness and precision of advertising graphics, being images that are, at the same time, ironical, charged with allusions, with both verbal and visual puns, yet withdrawn and reticent.

If Picabia's visual images were often detached in the Duchamp manner, other aspects of his activities were less so. In his poetry and in his written statements, particularly when he later came to run his own magazine, *391*, in Barcelona and Paris, the *provacateur* appears, indeed on occasions a cultural terrorist, violent and destructive. Speaking of literature he has said, '. . . every page must explode, whether through seriousness, profundity, violence, nausea, the new, the eternal, annihilating nonsense, enthusiasm for principles or the way it is printed. Art must be unaesthetic in the extreme, useless and impossible to justify.'

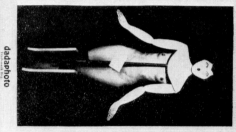

dadaphoto

# EYE-COVER  ART-COVER  CORSET-COVER
## AUTHORIZATION

**NEW YORK-DADA:**

You ask for authorization to name your periodical Dada. But Dada belongs to everybody. I know excellent people who have the name Dada. Mr. Jean Dada; Mr. Gaston de Dada; Fr. Picabia's dog is called Zizi de Dada; in G. Ribemont-Dessaigne's play, the pope is likewise named Zizi de Dada. I could cite dozens of examples. Dada belongs to everybody. Like the idea of God or of the tooth-brush. There are people who are very dada, more dada; there are dadas everywere all over and iit very individual. Like God and the tooth1brush (an excellent invention, by the way).

Dada is a new type; a mixture of man, naphthaline, sponge, animal made of ebonite and beefsteak, prepared with soap for cleansing the brain. Good teeth are the making of the stomach and beautiful teeth are the making of a charming smile. Halleluiah of ancient oil and injection of rubber.

There is nothing abnormal about my choice of Dada for the name of my review. In Switzerland I was in the company of friends and was hunting the dictionary for a word appropriate to the sonorities of all languages. Night was upon us when a green hand placed its ugliness on the page of Larousse—pointing very precisely to Dada—my choice was made. I lit a cigarette and drank a demitasse.

For Dada was to say nothing and to lead to no explanation of this offshoot of relationship which is not a dogma nor a school, but rather a constellation of individuals and of free facets.

Dada existed before us (the Holy Virgin) but one cannot deny its magical power to add to this already existing spirit and impulses of penetration and diversity that characterizes its present form.

There is nothing more incomprehensible than Dada.

Nothing more indefinable.

With the best will in the world I cannot tell you what I think of it.

The journalists who say that Dada is a pretext are right, but it is a pretext for something I do not know.

Dada has penetrated into every hamlet, Dada is the best paying concern of the day.

Therefore, Madam, be on your guard and realize that a really dada product is a different thing from a glossy label.

Dada abolishes "nuances." Nuances do not exist in words but only in some atrophied brains whose cells are too jammed. Dada is an anti "nuance" cream. The simple motions that serve as signs for deaf-mutes are quite adequate to express the four or five mysteries we have discovered within 7 or 8,000 years. Dada offers all kinds of advantages. Dada will soon be able to boast of having shown people that to say "right" instead of "left" is neither less nor too logical, that red and valise are the same thing; that 2765 — 34; that "fool" is a merit; that yes — no. Strong influences are making themselves felt in politics, in commerce, in language. The whole world and what's in it has slid to the left along with us. Dada has inserted its syringe into hot bread, to speak allegorically into language. Little by little (large by large) it destroys it. Everything collapses with logic. And we shall see certain liberties we constantly take in the sphere of sentiment, social life, morals, once more become normal standards. These liberties no longer will be looked upon as crime, but as itches.

I will close with a little international song: Order from the publishing house "La Sirene" 7 rue Pasquier, Paris, DADAGLOBE, the work of dadas from all over the world. Tell your bookseller that this book will soon be out of print. You will have many agreable surprises.

Read Dadaglobe if you have troubles. Dadaglobe is in press. Here are some of its colloborators:

Paul Citroen (Amsterdam); Baader Daimonides; R. Hausmann; W. Heartfield; H. Hoech; R. Huelsenbeck; G. Grosz; Fried Hardy Worm (Berlin); Clement Pansaers (Bruxelles); Mac Robber (Calcutta); Jacques Edwards (Chili); Baargeld, Armada v. Dulgedalzen, Max Ernst, F. Haubrich (Cologne); K. Schwitters (Hannovre); J. K. Bonset (Leyde); Guillermo de Torre (Madrid); Gino Cantarelli; E. Bacchi, A. Fiozzi (Mantoue); Krusenitch (Moscou); A. Vagts (Munich); W. C. Arensberg, Gabrielle Buffet, Marcel Duchamp; Adon Lacroix; Baroness v. Loringhoven; Man Ray; Joseph Stella; E. Varese; A. Stieglitz; M. Hartley; C. Kahler (New York); Louis Aragon; C. Brancusi; André Breton; M. Buffet; S. Charchoune; J. Crotti; Suzanne Duchamp; Paul Eluard; Benjamin Peret; Francis Picabia; G. Ribemont-Dessaignes; J. Rigaut, Soubeyran; Ph. Soupault. Tristan Tzara (Paris); Melchior Vischer (Prague); J. Evola (Rome); Arp; S. Taeuber (Zurich).

The incalculable number of pages of reproductions and of text is a guaranty of the success of the book. Articles of luxury, of prime necessity, articles indispensable to hygiene and to the heart, toilet articles of an intimate nature.

Such, Madame, do we prepare for Dadaglobe; for you need look no further than to the use of articles prepared without Dada to account for the fact that the skin of your heart is chapped; that the so precious enamel of your intelligence is cracking; also for the presence of those tiny wrinkles still imperceptible but nevertheless disquieting.

All this and much else in Dadaglobe.          TRISTAN TZARA.

**Man Ray** *The Rope Dancer Accompanies Herself with Her Shadows* 1916
oil on canvas 52 × 73$\frac{3}{8}$ in.
Museum of Modern Art, New York, gift of G. David Thompson

70

In New York, as elsewhere, there were individuals who went beyond questions of art and anti-art, who took the idea of the Dada *geste* totally into their lives, who seemed to live their lives every moment according to Dada principles. Such a person was the extraordinary Arthur Cravan, Dada *provocateur par excellence*; boxer, poet and sailor, he was of English origin, claiming to be the nephew of Oscar Wilde. He first came to sight on the Dada horizon in 1912 when he was living in Paris and publishing a small magazine called *Maintenant.* This publication appears to have been a clear forerunner of the aggressive post-war Parisian journals like *361* and *Littérature*. Cravan engaged in hell-raising of all sorts, notably in an article he wrote in 1914 attacking the Independent Exhibition which ended in Apollinaire's challenging him to a duel. At the outbreak of war he decided that he was not going to be personally involved and disappeared to resurface in Barcelona two years later. Somehow he had managed to cross half a dozen belligerent countries without being discovered or arrested, paradoxically avoiding personal involvement in the war by wandering illegally as an individual across the thick of it in Central Europe.

It was in Barcelona that he engaged in his famous fight with Jack Johnson, challenging the reigning world heavyweight champion, but he did not do too well. There are conflicting reports, but it seems likely that he anticipated defeat by appearing in the ring somewhat drunk. 1917 found him in New York, where he made his own personal contribution to the Exhibition of Independent Painters, already marked by sensational incident in that a famous quarrel developed around the jury's refusal to hang Duchamp's entry, *Fountain*, the urinal signed enigmatically by a certain Mr R. Mutt, the work of which Duchamp has stated, 'Whether Mr Mutt with his own hands made the fountain or not has no importance. He *chose* it. He took an ordinary article of life, placed it so that its useful significance disappeared under the new title and point of view—created a new thought for that object.' As part of the whole programme of the exhibition, it was arranged that Cravan should deliver a lecture on the 'new art', particularly as he had been in close touch with the earlier activities in Paris and elsewhere. Elaborate arrangements were made and a very elegant audience was solicited; arriving late for the lecture, clearly somewhat the worse for drink, he began to insult his audience of smart Park Avenue ladies with some of the choicest obscenities of the English language, while slowly taking his clothes off. Cravan's life was one long Dada *geste*, a non-stop provocation of society. His death was entirely in character; he disappeared without trace one day in 1918 while sailing a small boat in the Gulf of Mexico.

A different Dada quality was manifested by Man Ray, the quality of extreme curiosity, of tireless experiment. Originally trained as a painter, Man Ray fell under the influence of Stieglitz and became a photographer, in which medium his most significant contribution to Dada was presented. With his invention of the 'rayograph', a photographic image achieved without a camera by means of exposing sensitized paper to light with objects and cut-outs producing images, he created works of hallucinatory power and opened up a whole area of photographic technique. Though it should be noted at this point that Christian Schad, a hitherto somewhat neglected member of the Zürich group, independently stumbled upon analogous techniques which Tzara called, in one of the more painful Dada puns, 'Schadographs'.

As well as his activities in photography and painting, Man Ray created innumerable enigmatic objects which were essentially 'assisted readymades', the best known of which are possibly *Gift*, the somewhat sadistic flat-iron studded with tintacks, the *Enigma of Isidore Ducasse*, a mysterious packaged object which, though it could not be seen, was in fact a sewing-machine, drawing a direct analogy with Ducasse Lautréamont's famous poetici mage about the 'chance encounter on a dissecting table' of an umbrella and a sewing-machine, and finally, the *Object to be Destroyed*, a metronome with a ticking, unwinking eye attached by a paper clip, which two young visitors to an exhibition took literally and destroyed with pistol shots.

# Arp

## Aus „Die Wolkenpumpe"

lachende tiere schäumen aus eisernen kannen die wolkenwalzen drängen die tiere aus ihren kernen und steinen nackt stehen hufe auf steinalten steinen mäuschenstill bei zweigen und gräten geweihe spiesen schneekugeln auf stühlen galoppieren könige in die berge und predigen das dezemberhorn läßt strohbrücken nieder bringt eisenbriefe lautlos und gut hörbar in der eisflasche gefrieren die turteltauben

nie hat der er den schweißbrüchigen bergwald durch schwarz harz steigen empor und sind leise in feinen lufttreppen in stengeln in der eisernen rüstung des vogels dreht sich das kind über feuerroter troika noch die leichen der engel mit goldenen eggen geeggt noch die büsche mit brennenden vögeln getränkt noch auf wachsschlitten über das gärende sommereis gefahren noch vorhänge aus schwarzen fischen zugezogen noch in kleinen gläsern luft in die kastelle getragen noch vögel aus wasser gestrickt geschweige auf stelzen über die wolken auf säulen über die meere

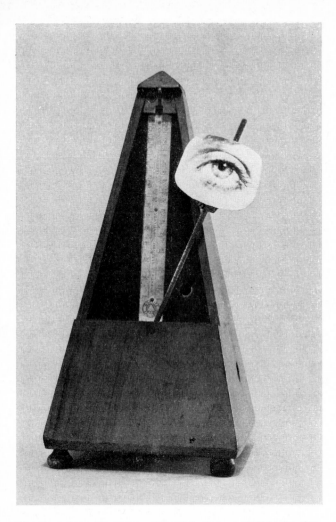

**Man Ray** *Indestructible Object or Object to be Destroyed* 1964 (replica after a 1923 original destroyed in 1957) metronome with cut-out photograph of eye on pendulum $8\frac{7}{8} \times 4\frac{3}{8} \times 4\frac{5}{8}$ in.
Museum of Modern Art, New York, James Thrall Soby Fund

*Opposite*
*Der Zeltweg* 1919 page

## Berlin—political commitment

Berlin, in 1918, was absolutely different in character from any other city where Dada took hold: the pistol shots were real and serious. In Zürich and New York, Dada attacked the established order on an intellectual plane, as it were—but in Berlin, at the close of the war, there was a genuine and full-blown, if somewhat short-lived, revolution. There was street fighting; soldiers' and workers' councils, factory soviets and syndicalist communes convened under the Communist, Anarchist and Spartakist banners; all the left-wing intelligentsia threw themselves into fervent activity—Dada particularly, for here at last, it seemed, special talents for subversion could find concrete goals, their activity be harnessed to the dawning new society.

Even during the war years, the Berlin artists and potential revolutionaries were permitted an amount of freedom that is astonishing when one considers the ferocious censorship of a very few years later. The Café des Westerns, which later became under a different management the Café Grossenwahn, was the centre for the writers and painters who opposed the political structure of the Kaiser's Germany. The magazine *Die Aktion* (upon the wall of whose office was the ironic defeatist placard stating that 'only a bad harvest can save us'), edited by Franz Pfemfert, was able to print poetry and prose directly critical of the war, as was also *Sturm* edited by Herwarth Walden. And from 1916 the two Herzfelde brothers published a strongly left-wing polemical journal, *Neue Jugend*. Wieland Herzfelde was a writer, poet and political commentator, while his brother Helmut who, as an anti-nationalist gesture, anglicized his name to John Heartfield, was later to become one of the most important figures among the German Dadaists.

At the same time, the painter Raoul Hausmann and the poet Franz Jung were responsible for the anarchist publication *Die Freie Strasse*, while Johannes Baader, one of the most provocative anti-establishment figures, and the savagely satirical painter George Grosz were actively undermining the social assumptions

Direktion r. hausmann

№ 2

DER

# DADA

Preis 1 Mark

*dada siegt!*

*Tretet dada bei.*

**John Heartfield** *War and Corpses—last hope of the rich* 1932 photomontage
Collection Mrs John Heartfield, Berlin

**George Grosz** *Was ist Dada?* from *Der Dada* no. 2 about 1920

of the period. When Richard Huelsenbeck returned from Zürich in
1917, bearing the message of Dada, he was, as it were, the lit
taper for an already prepared explosive charge beneath a confused and shaky society.

After an initial meeting in April 1918, in which he violently
attacked Expressionism, Cubism and abstract art, Huelsenbeck
read out a manifesto defining Dada, and launched it as an official
movement with a specific policy as opposed to the collective of
individual contributions that comprised the Zürich situation. This
manifesto, signed also by Tzara, Arp, Janco, Ball and others,
stated that:

Dada is a CLUB, founded in Berlin, which you can join without
commitments. In this club every man is chairman and every man

stbildnis von George Grosz

Was ist **dada**?

Eine Kunst?, Eine Philosophie? eine Politik?
**Eine Feuerversicherung?**

Oder: Staatsreligion?

ist dada wirklich **Energie?**

oder ist es **Garnichts**, d. h.
**alles?**

noch an der paranoischen Idee laborierte, dass er der Präsident der Welt sei, lehnte meinen Vorschlag ab und kam selbst mit seinem Friedensangebot heraus, was natürlich gänzlich verfehlt war. Ich ging jetzt direkt an die Front nach Flandern, setzte mich an die Spitze der Truppen, aber die Etappe fiel mir in den Rücken, man schleppte mich in den Jusizpalast der Vierten Armee-Inspektion nach Gent, internierte mich in der Kaiser-Wilhelm-Kaserne und die Folgen kennt man. Czernin schrieb in Wien seinen geheimen Bericht an den Kaiser Karl; der Bericht gelangte in die Hände der Entente; Wilson wurde ersucht, dem deutschen Volke klar zu machen, dass der Präsident von Amerika die Sorge für sein Wohl übernommen und jede weitere Bemühung in Deutschland überflüssig sei. Vergebens machte ich am 19. September 17 meinen Besuch in Kreuznach. Hindendorf und Ludenburg erklärten mir beide gleichzeitig, meine geistigen Tanks seien ganz ungefährlich, und sie übernähmen nach wie vor jede Garantie für den Sieg. Gegen diese Verblendung gab es kein Mittel mehr. So trat ich im Frühjahr 1918 zum Dadaismus über. Man ernannte mich zum Oberdada. Aber statt dass man am 9. November vernünftig geworden wäre, und, nun die Bahn frei war, mir das ehemalige kaiserliche Schloss eingeräumt und mich zum Diktator des Proletariats ernannt hätte, lehnte Liebknecht die deutsche Präsidentschaft, die ihm Adolf Hoffmann auf dem Balkon des Schlosses anbot, ab; am 17. November versuchte ich im Dom eine letzte Klärung der Sachlage; Adolf Hoffmann, der damals im Kultusministerium sass, und zu dessen Ressort die Angelegenheit gehörte, liess mich im Stich, und so wurden Karl Liebknecht und Rosa Luxemburg am 15. Januar im Edenhotel ermordet. Dann folgte ein Schlag auf den andern. Am 7. Mai wurde der Friedensvertrag in Versailles überreicht, nachdem ich am 19. April vergeblich im Reichsministerium persönlich meine Karte abgegeben und festgestellt hatte, dass ich nicht tot bin, auch wenn die Presse mich für tot erklärt hat. Aber wieder redete ich vergeblich. Scheidemann und Ebert wussten alles besser, bis zum 28. Juni. Doch inzwischen war unser

ihre Pappgeschosse zu machen — sie sind Eigenschaften einer Jugend, die es niemals vorstanden hat, jung zu sein. Der Expressionismus, der im Ausland gefunden, in Deutschland nach beliebter Manier eine fette Idylle und Erwartung guter Pension geworden ist, hat mit dem Streben tätiger Menschen nichts mehr zu tun. Die Unterzeichner dieses Manifests haben sich unter dem Streitruf

# DADA!!!!

zur Propaganda einer Kunst gesammelt, von der sie die Verwirklichung neuer Ideale erwarten. Was ist nun der **DADAISMUS?**

Das Wort Dada symbolisiert das primitivste Verhältnis zur umgebenden Wirklichkeit, mit dem Dadaismus tritt eine neue Realität in ihre Rechte. Das Leben erscheint als ein simultanes Gewirr von Geräuschen, Farben und geistigen Rhytmen, das in die dadaistische Kunst unbeirrt mit allen sensationellen Schreien und Fiebern seiner verwegenen Alltagspsyche und in seiner gesamten brutalen Realität übernommen wird. Hier ist der scharf markierte Scheideweg, der den Dadaismus von allen bisherigen Kunstrichtungen und vor allem von dem **FUTURISMUS** trennt, den kürzlich Schwachköpfe als eine neue Auflage impressionistischer Realisierung aufgefaßt haben. Der Dadaismus steht zum erstenmal dem Leben nicht mehr ästhetisch gegenüber, indem er alle Schlagworte von Ethik, Kultur und Innerlichkeit, die nur Mäntel für schwache Muskeln sind, in seine Bestandteile zerfetzt.

Das
## BRUITISTISCHE Gedicht

schildert eine Trambahn wie sie ist, die Essenz der Trambahn mit dem Gähnen des Rentiers Schulze und dem Schrei der Bremsen.

Das
## SIMULTANISTISCHE Gedicht

lehrt den Sinn des Durcheinanderjagens aller Dinge, während Herr Schulze liest, fährt der Balkanzug über die Brücke bei Nisch, ein Schwein jammert im Keller des Schlächters Nuttke.

Das
## STATISCHE Gedicht

macht die Worte zu Individuen, aus den drei Buchstaben Wald, tritt der Wald mit seinen Baumkronen, Försterlivreen und Wildsauen, vielleicht tritt auch eine Pension heraus, vielleicht Bellevue oder Bella vista. Der Dadaismus führt zu unerhörten neuen Möglichkeiten und Ausdrucksformen aller Künste. Er hat den Kubismus zum Tanz auf der Bühne gemacht, er hat die **BRUITISTISCHE** Musik der Futuristen (deren rein italienische Angelegenheit er nicht verallgemeinern will) in allen Ländern Europas propagiert. Das Wort Dada weist zugleich auf die Internationalität der Bewegung,

**Richard Huelsenbeck** 'Dadaistisches Manifest' 1918

die an keine Grenzen, Religionen oder Berufe gebunden ist. Dada ist der internationale Ausdruck dieser Zeit, die große Fronde der Kunstbewegungen, der künstlerische Reflex aller dieser Offensiven, Friedenskongresse, Balgereien am Gemüsemarkt, Soupers im Esplanade etc. etc. Dada will die Benutzung des

## neuen Materials in der Malerei.

Dada ist ein **CLUB,** der in Berlin gegründet worden ist, in den man eintreten kann, ohne Verbindlichkeiten zu übernehmen. Hier ist jeder Vorsitzender und jeder kann sein Wort abgeben, wo es sich um künstlerische Dinge handelt. Dada ist nicht ein Vorwand für den Ehrgeiz einiger Literaten (wie unsere Feinde glauben machen möchten) Dada ist eine Geistesart, die sich in jedem Gespräch offenbaren kann, sodaß man sagen muß: dieser ist ein **DADAIST** — jener nicht; der Club Dada hat deshalb Mitglieder in allen Teilen der Erde, in Honolulu so gut wie in New-Orleans und Meseritz. Dadaist sein kann unter Umständen heißen, mehr Kaufmann, mehr Parteimann als Künstler sein — nur zufällig Künstler sein — Dadaist sein, heißt, sich von den Dingen werfen lassen, gegen jede Sedimentsbildung sein, ein Moment auf einem Stuhl gesessen, heißt, das Leben in Gefahr gebracht haben (Mr. Wengs zog schon den Revolver aus der Hosentasche). Ein Gewebe zerreißt sich unter der Hand, man sagt ja zu einem Leben, das durch Verneinung höher will. Ja-sagen — Nein-sagen: das gewaltige Hokuspokus des Daseins beschwingt die Nerven des echten Dadaisten — so liegt er, so jagt er, so radelt er — halb Pantagruel, halb Franziskus und lacht und lacht. Gegen die ästhetisch-ethische Einstellung! Gegen die blutleere Abstraktion des Expressionismus! Gegen die weltverbessernden Theorien literarischer Hohlköpfe! Für den Dadaismus in Wort und Bild, für das dadaistische Geschehen in der Welt. Gegen dies Manifest sein, heißt Dadaist sein!

**Tristan Tzara. Franz Jung. George Grosz. Marcel Janco. Richard Huelsenbeck. Gerhard Preiß. Raoul Hausmann.**

**O. Lüthy. Fréderic Glauser. Hugo Ball. Pierre Albert Birot. Maria d'Arezzo Gino Cantarelli. Prampolini. R. van Rees. Madame van Rees. Hans Arp. G. Thäuber. Andrée Morosini. François Mombello-Pasquati.**

Von diesem Manifest sind 25 Exemplare mit den Unterschriften der Berliner Vertreter des Dadaismus versehen worden und zum Preise von fünf Mark bei Richard Huelsenbeck, Berlin-Charlottenburg, Kantstr. 118, III, zu beziehen. Alle Anfragen und Bestellungen bitte man an die gleiche Adresse zu richten.

Leiter der Bewegung in der Schweiz: Tristan Tzara, Zürich, Zeltweg 83 (Administration du Mouvement Dada F. Arp), Leiter in Skandinavien: Francis Morton, Stockholm, Marholms Gaden 14.

can have his say in artistic matters. Dada is not a pretext for the ambition of a few literary men (as our enemies would have us believe), Dada is a state of mind that can be revealed in any conversation whatever, so that you are compelled to say : this man is a DADAIST—that man is not ; the Club Dada consequently has members all over the world, in Honolulu as well as in New Orleans and Meseritz. Under certain circumstances to be a Dadaist may mean to be more a businessman, more a political partisan than an artist—to be an artist only by accident—to be a Dadaist means to let oneself be thrown by things, to oppose all sedimentation ; to sit in a chair for a single moment is to risk one's life.

Berlin was entirely different from Zürich, spiritually and politically worlds away. After years of war which resulted in a staggering death roll, a revolution was being fought out in the suddenly open climate engendered by the armistice, yet it was a revolution that was indistinct and inconclusive. The artists identified with the revolutionary left perhaps without being quite clear what were the issues involved and what the left might lead to. Dadaism and Communism were linked, but in a romantic rather than an ideological manner.

Huelsenbeck describes his return from Switzerland in his *En Avant Dada*, the first history of Dada, published in 1920 :

I felt as though I had left a smug fat idyll for a street full of electric signs, shouting hawkers and auto horns. In Zürich the international profiteers sat in the restaurants with well-filled wallets and rosy cheeks, ate with their knives and smacked their lips in a merry hurrah for the countries that were bashing each other's skulls in. Berlin was the city of tightened stomachs, of mounting, thundering hunger, where hidden rage was transformed into a boundless money-lust, and men's minds were concentrating more and more on questions of naked existence.

In Zürich, Tzara was saying that 'Dada ne signifie rien', while in Germany, Dada 'went out and found an adversary'.

Huelsenbeck and Hausmann formed a 'Dadaist Revolutionary Central Council' in which a consciously political position was taken up, but it was a political position such as had never before been proposed. 'Dadaism demands', states a manifesto :

1 The international revolutionary union of all creative and intellectual men and women on the basis of radical Communism ;
2 The introduction of progressive unemployment through

*Club Dada* 1918 cover

PrOSpekT
des VErlags

R Hülsenbeck

freie Straße

f juNg man

r. haus

Heraus
gebeR

*Club Dada* 1918 page

comprehensive mechanization of every field of activity. Only by unemployment does it become possible for the individual to achieve certainty as to the truth of life and finally become accustomed to experience;

**Raoul Hausmann** *Dada Milchstrasse* 1919 poster
Collection Timothy Baum, New York

3 The immediate expropriation of property (socialization) and the communal feeding of all; further the erection of cities of light, the gardens of which will belong to society as a whole and prepare man for a state of freedom.

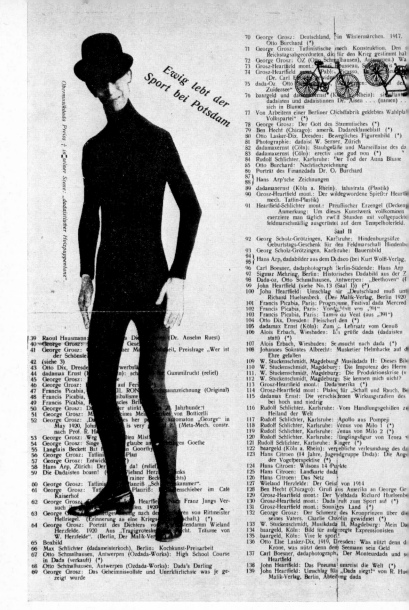

Ewig lebt der Sport bei Potsdam

Obermusikdada Preß + in seiner Szene: „dadaistischer Holzpuppentanz".

70 George Grosz: Deutschland, ein Wintermärchen. 1917.
   Otto Burchard (*)
71 George Grosz: Tatimistische mech. Konstruktion. Der
   Reichstagsabgeordneten, die für den Krieg gestimmt hat
72 George Grosz: OZ (Otto Schmalhausen), Antwerpen.) Wa
73 Grosz-Heartfield mont.: Henri Rousseau, Se...... is s
74 Grosz-Heartfield mont.: Tablo..... Picasso, ...... ien
   (Dr. Carl Einstein)
75 dada-Oz: Otto ..................... en ......... des
   Zuidersee"
76 baargeld und dada...ernst (Köln a. Rhein): simultan
   dadaisten und dadaistinnen Dr. Aisen ... (namen) ...
   sich in Blumen
77 Von Arbeitern einer Berliner Clichéfabrik geklebtes Wahlpla
   Volkspartei" (*)
78 George Grosz: Der Gott des Stammtisches (*)
79 Ben Hecht (Chicago): amerik. Dadareklameblatt (*)
80 Otto Lasker-Dix, Dresden: Bewegliches Figurenbild (*)
81 Photographie: dadaist W. Serner, Zürich
82 dadamaxernst (Cöln): Staubgefäße und Marseillaise des da
83 dadamaxernst (Cöln): erectiv sine gud non (*)
84 Rudolf Schlichter, Karlsruhe: Der Tod der Anna Blume
85 Otto Burchard: Nachtischzeichnung
86 Porträt des Finanzdada Dr. O. Burchard
87
88 Hans Arp'sche Zeichnungen
89 dadamaxernust (Köln a. Rhein). falustrata (Plastik)
90 Grosz-Heartfield mont.: Der wildegwordene Spießer Heartfi
   mech. Tatlin-Plastik)
91 Heartfield-Schlichter mont.: Preußischer Erzengel (Decken
   Anmerkung: Um dieses Kunstwerk vollkommen
   exerziere man täglich zwei Stunden mit vollgepackte
   feldmarschmäßig ausgerüstet auf dem Tempelhoferfeld.

Saal II

92 Georg Scholz-Grötzingen, Karlsruhe: Hindenburgsülze.
   Geburtstags-Geschenk für den Feldmarschall Hindenb
93 Georg Scholz-Grötzingen, Karlsruhe: Bauernbild
94
95
96 Carl Boesner, dadaphotograph Berlin-Südende: Hans Arp
97 Sigmar Mehring, Berlin: Historisches Dadabild aus der Z
98 Dada-oz, Otto Schmalhausen, Antwerpen: „Beethoven" (*)
99 John Heartfield (siehe No.13 (Saal I)) (*)
100 John Heartfield: Umschlag zur „Deutschland muß unt
   Richard Huelsenbeck (Den Malik-Verlag, Berlin 1920)
101 Francis Picabia, Paris: Programme, Festival dada Merced
102 Francis Picabia, Paris: Vorstellung von „301"
103 Francis Picabia, Paris: Tam-o' du Veut (aus „301")
104 Otto Dix, Dresden: Fleischerladen (*)
105 dadamax Ernst (Köln): Zum ... Lehrsatz vom Genuß
106 Alois Erbach, Wiesbaden: Ich grüße dada (dadaisten
107 Alois Erbach, Wiesbaden: Sehnsucht nach dada (*)
108 Johannes Sokrates Albrecht: Musketier Helmhacke auf d
   Ehre gefallen
109 W. Stuckenschmidt, Magdeburg Musikdada II: Dieses Bile
110 W. Stuckenschmidt, Magdeburg: Die Impotenz des Herrm
111 W. Stuckenschmidt, Magdeburg: Die Produktionskrise (v
112 W. Stuckenschmidt, Magdeburg: Sie kennen mich nicht?
113 Grosz-Heartfield mont.: Dada-merika (*)
114 Grosz-Heartfield mont.: Plakat für „Schall und Rauch, Be
115 dadamax Ernst: Die verschiedenen Wirkungsradien des
   bei hoch und niedrig
116 Rudolf Schlichter, Karlsruhe: Vom Handlungsgehilfen zu
   Heiland der Welt
117 Rudolf Schlichter, Karlsruhe: Apollo aus Pompeji
118 Rudolf Schlichter, Karlsruhe: Venus von Milo 1 (*)
119 Rudolf Schlichter, Karlsruhe: Venus von Milo 2 (*)
120 Rudolf Schlichter, Karlsruhe: Jünglingsfigur von Tenea (*
121 Rudolf Schlichter, Karlsruhe: Finger (*)
122 baargeld (Köln a. Rhein): vergebliche verleumdung des dada
123 Hans Citroen (14 Jahre, Jugendgruppe Dada): Die Ange
   der Vogelperspektive (*)
124 Hans Citroen: Wilsons 14 Punkte
125 Hans Citroen: Landkarte dada
126 Hans Citroen: Das Netz
127 Wieland Herzfelde: Der Geist von 1914
128 Ben Hecht (Chicago): Gruß aus Amerika an George Gr
129 Grosz-Heartfield mont.: Der Weltdada Richard Huelsenbec
130 Grosz-Heartfield mont.: Dada ruft zum Sport auf (*)
131 Grosz-Heartfield mont.: Sonniges Land (*)
132 George Grosz: Der Schmerz des Kronprinzen über die
   seines Vaters, Charlie Chaplin gewidmet (*)
133 W. Stuckenschmidt, Musikdada II, Magdeburg: Mein Da
134 baargeld, Köln: Bild für aufgeregte Expressionisten
135 baargeld, Köln: Vive le sport!
136 Otto Else Lasker-Dix, 1919, Dresden: Was nützt denn d
   Krone, was nützt denn dem Seemann sein Geld
137 Carl Boesner, dadaphotograph, Der Monteurdada und se
   Heartfield
138 John Heartfield: Das Pneuma umreist die Welt (*)
139 John Heartfield: Umschlag für „Dada siegt" von R. Hue
   Malik-Verlag, Berlin, Abteilung dada

39 Raoul Hausmann: ...... Die ...... (Dr. Anselm Ruest)
40 George Grosz: ......................... Gese
41 George Grosz: ............. her Ma...heit, Preisfrage „Wer ist
   der Schönste ...
42 (siehe 3)
43 Otto Dix, Dresde: ...............werbsl
44 dadamax Ernst (...............an): sch ...... Gummifrucht (relief)
45 George Grosz: ...........................
46 George Grosz: ............. auf Feri ...
47 Francis Picabia, ...... IL RON ...... schmannzeichnung (Original)
48 Francis Picabia, ........... hibalisme
49 Francis Picabia, ........... scles Bri
50 George Grosz: D ........... er stinkt ...... Jahrhunde
51 George Grosz: ........... eines Mei ...... en von Botticelli
52 George Grosz: ...... her p ...... utomaton „George" in
   May 1920, Join ......... is very di ...... (Meta-Mech. constr.
   nach Prof. R. H...
53 George Grosz: Weg ........... ten Mist
54 George Grosz: Singe ...... glaube an ...... ligen Goethe
55 Langlais Beckett Bst R ...... Goorthy
56 George Grosz: Tatlini ...... Plan
57 George Grosz: Entwick ...........
58 Hans Arp, Zürich: Der ...... da! (relief ...
59 Die Dadaisten boxen! (...... Wieland Herz ...... finks
   ...... rainer Beck ...... chts)
60 George Grosz: Tatlini ...... Plaurß ...... „Sch ...... skammer")
61 George Grosz: Tat ...... Plaurß: ...... enschieber im Café
   Kaiserhof
62 George Grosz ........................ Heartfiel ...... Nach Franz Jungs Ver-
   such ...................... n. 1920 ...
63 George Gr ........... ung nach de ...... ren von Rittmeister
   Hellriegel. (Erinnerungen an eine Kriegs ...
64 George Grosz: Porträt des Dichters vo ...... estandamm Wieland
   Herzfelde. 1920 Aus „Tragigroteske ...... ucht. Träume von
   W. Herzfelde". (Berlin, Der Malik-Ver ...
65 Boxbild
66 Max Schlichter (dadameisterkoch), Berlin: Kochkunst-Preisarbeit
67 Otto Schmalhausen, Antwerpen (Ozdada-Works): High School Course
   in Dada (verkauft) (*)
68 Otto Schmalhausen, Antwerpen (Ozdada-Works): Dada's Darling
69 George Grosz: Das Geheimnisvollste und Unerklärlichste was je gezeigt wurde

Catalogue of the First International Dada Fair, Berlin 1920 centre page

140 Grosz-Heartfield: Einband der politischen Mappe von George Grosz
„Gott mit uns!" Der Malik-Verlag, Berlin

141 George Grosz: Photoporträt von Otto Else Lasker-Dix, Dresden

142 George Grosz: Photoporträt von Mutzdada I

143 Grosz-Heartfield mont.: Der deutsche Dummkopf in der Welt voran.
Reklameplastik

144 Raoul Hausmann: Abstrakte Spielerei

145 Georg Kobbe: Umschlag für „Menschen und Korruption" von W.
Petry. Leon Hirsch Verlag

146 Georg Kobbe: Schall und Rauch-Fantasie

147 max ernst, Cöln: nationalcodex und delicateß-index und dada baargeld

150 John Heartfield: Neue Jugend, Wochenausgabe No. 1
151 }                    (siehe Saal 1 No. 13) (*)

152 John Heartfield: „Leben und Treiben in Universal-City, 12 Uhr 5
mittags". Besitzer Lämmle; Kalifornien (*)

153 Ehrenporträt von Charlie Chaplin.

154 Georg Koch (gen.: Der Maskenkoch): Transformation

155 Maud E. Grosz: Das Waisenkind (Kissen) (*) Die erste amerikanischen
156 Maud E. Grosz: Mr. Curtis reist (Kissen) (*) Kissen in der Welt

157 John Heartfield: Umschlag für „Phantastische Gebete" von R. Huelsenbeck. (Der Malik-Verlag, Berlin)

158 A. Baader, Oberdada, Präsident des Erd- und Weltballs, Inhaber des Weltgerichts, Wirklicher Geheimer Vorsitzender des interfederalistischen ober-
dadaistischen Völkerbunds, Repräsentant von Lehrer Hagendorfs
Lesepult, ehemals Architekt und Schriftsteller: Reiseausstattung des
Oberdadas bei seiner ersten Flucht aus dem Irrenhaus, am 17. September 1899. (Dada-Relique. Historisch)

159–160 B. Baader, Oberdada: Acht Seiten aus dem Buch des Weltgerichts
C. (*) (HADO = Handbuch des Oberdadaismus). Erste Ausgabe vom
D. (*) 26. Juni 1, 3 Uhr nachmittags. Das Buch ist am 16. Juli 1 a
E. (*) Weimar vom Oberdada selbst der Nationalversammlung zur
F.       Geschenk geboten worden. Der Abgeordnete Friedrich
G.       Naumann, der das Geschenk übermitteln sollte, hat sich ge-
H.       weigert und ist deshalb gestorben.
I.       Das Material der Seiten besteht aus historischen Zeitungsblättern.
         Seite B ist das äußere, Seite C das innere Titelblatt.

Die zweite Ausgabe des HADO ist am 28. Juni 2 erschienen.
Sie liegt nicht öffentlich aus, kann aber beim Generaldada
Dr. Otto Burchard, Exzellenz, eingesehen werden.

167 M. Baader, Oberdada: Meine Visitkarte.

168 N. Baader, Oberdada: Geschäftskarte der Correspondenz Hähne.

169 O. Baader, Oberdada: Warum verdreht Carnegie seine Augen?

170 P. Baader am Galgen.

171 Q. Entwurf zu einem Tierparadies im Jardin d'Acclimation, Paris.
(Enthält die Gelasse für alle französischen und deutschen
Dadaisten, im Stil Hagenbeck, ohne Gitter.)

172 R. Der Club Dada in der Blauen Milchstraße. Begründung der neuen
Zeitrechnung durch die Vorsitzenden des Anationalen Rats der
unbezahlten Arbeiter (ARDUA) Baader und Hausmann. Be-
schluß: korporativ Reklame zu machen für Lehrer Hagendorfs
Lesepult (Kein Mensch liest; kein Kind geht in die Schule ohne
Lehrer Hagendorfs Lesepult). Käuflich an der Kasse der Dada-
Ausstellung zum Preis von M. 7.75.

173 W. Bekanntmachungen des Oberdada. Man nehme das ausgelegte Buch,
klappe es auf und stecke die Rückendeckel in die beiden eisernen
Halten. (Das Lesepult ist gebrauchsfertig. (Das ausgelegte Buch
ist das Handbuch des Islam mit dem Bildnis des Oberdada (Allah
ist groß aber der Oberdada ist noch größer). (Seiten aus dem
Wolken gefallen im Café Josty, Berlin, Potsdamer Platz am
17. Mai 1). Bildnis aufgenommen am 29. Oktober 1914 bei
A. Wertheim. Eintritt der Türkei in den Weltkrieg. Bestellungen
auf Lehrer Hagendorfs Lesepult beliebe man, wenn die Kasse
kein Vorrat ist, in den goldenen Teller zu legen.

174 Z. Das große Plasto-Dio-Dada-Drama:
DEUTSCHLANDS GROESSE UND UNTERGANG
durch Lehrer Hagendorf
oder
Die phantastische Lebensgeschichte
des Oberdada
Verlegt bei PAUL STEEGEMANN, ERNST ROWOHLT und KURT
WOLFF (Hannover, Berlin und München).
Dadaistische Monumentalarchitektur in fünf Stock-
werken, 3 Anlagen, einem Tunnel, 2 Aufzügen und einem
Cylinderabschluß.
Beschreibung der Stockwerke:
Das Erdgeschoß oder der Fußboden ist die prädestinierte Be-
stimmung vor der Geburt und gehört nicht zur Sache.
I. Stockwerk: Die Vorbereitung des Oberdada
II. Stockwerk: Die metaphysische Prüfung.
III. Stockwerk: Die Einweihung.
IV. Stockwerk: Der Weltkrieg.
V. Stockwerk: Weltrevolution.
Ueberstock: Der Cylinder schraubt sich in den Himmel und ver-
kündet die Widerauferstehung Deutschlands durch Lehrer Hagendorf
und sein Lesepult. Ewig.

Die im Katalog mit einem Sternchen (*) versehenen Arbeiten werden
nach Schluß der Ausstellung in der Société Anonyme, Inc., open its First
Exhibition of Modern Art, 19 East 47 th Street, New York ausgestellt. Es sind
dies die ersten deutschen Dada-Arbeiten, die in Amerika gezeigt werden.

This programme of extraordinary social and political idealism which foreshadows ideas held in certain areas of today's 'underground' and hippie communities was further defined in detail. The 'Central Council' also 'demanded' daily meals at public expense for all creative and intellectual people, the compulsory adherence of all priests and teachers to the 'Dadaist articles of faith', a state art centre, the adoption of a Simultaneist poem as a state prayer, the requisition of churches for performances of bruitist music and Dada poems, the organization of 150 circuses 'for the enlightenment of the proletariat', and the 'immediate regulation of all sexual relations according to the views of international Dadaism through establishment of a Dadaist sexual centre'.

The 'un-community' as Richter called it showed in general a remarkably vague grasp of political realities, despite the fact that Huelsenbeck had been named Commissar of Fine Arts during the brief Berlin revolution. The exceptions to this were the two Herzfelde brothers and Walter Mehring and George Grosz, who between them launched a whole series of satirical, violent and brilliant magazines, which were quickly banned by the authorities, only to pop up again under different titles: *Deadly Earnest, Every Man His Own Football, Rose-Coloured Spectacles, The Pill, Bankrupt, Adversary*, and many others. The publication and dissemination of these provocative journals entailed risks, not only from the authorities but also from the climate of violence prevailing at the time.

One of the most successful of these was *Every Man His Own Football*. Walter Mehring in his book *Berlin-Dada* describes how it was his idea to sell it in the streets from a sort of parade. They hired a bus and a band, complete with uniforms of frock-coats and top-hats, of the sort familiar from the funerals of ex-servicemen. The editorial staff of the magazine carried bundles of the magazine as if they were wreaths.

In the richer and more sophisticated areas of the city they were jeered at, but it was a different story when they entered the working-class areas of north and east Berlin.

*Der Dada* no. 2 about 1920 page

## He, he, Sie junger Mann
## Dada ist keine Kunstrichtung

# dadaco

### Kurt Wolff

Verlag in
München

*Dadaistischer Handatlas*

*Erscheint im Januar 1920*

## Grösstes
## Standard-Werk
### der Welt

Der Dadaco gibt den einzigen
authentischen Aufschluss über alle
Dadaisten der Gegenwart

Huelsenbeck
Hausmann-Baader
Mehring
Grosz-Heartfield

M. Höch

# Centralamt der **dada** istischen Bewegung in
**DEUTSCHLAND**

Charlottenburg, Kantstr. 118. Richard Huelsenbeck. Fernsprecher: Steinplatz 8998.

Through the streets of grey tenements, marked by the machine-gun fire of the Spartakus battles and ripped open by the howitzers of the Norske regime, the band was greeted with jubilation and applause as it played its two star turns, sentimental marching songs, 'Ich hatt' einen Kameraden' and 'Die Rasenbank am Elterngrab'. After the cannibal dances of the Kapp-putsch, more savage than Sophie Taeuber's marionettes, after the *danse macabre* of the Stahlhelm movement and its swastika ornaments which seem to have sprung straight out of Hans Arp's *Heraldry*, our Dada procession was greeted with a joy as spontaneous as the *on y danse* of the Paris mob before the Bastille. The phrase 'every man his own football' became a popular Berlin saying as an expression of contempt for authority and humbug.

The specific contribution of the Berlin Dadaists to the visual arts was to a great extent related to this political action. The invention of the *photomontage* was the unique development of this group. Typically, there is a lot of confusion and vehement counterclaims as to who 'invented' the technique of cutting out and pasting together photographic images. The Berlin Dadaists, Hausmann notes, 'were the first to use photography to create, from often totally disparate spatial and material elements, a new unity in which was revealed a visually and conceptually new image of the chaos of an age of war and revolution', while personally claiming innovation in the field. But so also do Grosz and Heartfield, who made images purporting to be postcards from the war which were visual arrangements cut up in 'such a way as to say in pictures what would have been banned by the censors if we had said it in words'.

This recurrent theme of claims and counterclaims for the ownership of a sort of 'patent' has, of course, bedevilled the whole history of modern art, and nowhere more than among the Dadaists. What is clear, though, is that the Berlin group as a whole contributed an entirely new technique to our visual experience, one that lies somewhere in the territory between the purely 'aesthetic' collages of the Cubists and the more poetic and 'surrealist' ones of Max Ernst. Hausmann, Heartfield and George Grosz, together with Hannah Hoch and Johannes Baader, produced a great many works in this idiom. Baader, who was originally trained as an architect, worked on a particularly large scale with torn posters,

**Richard Huelsenbeck** *Wozu war Dada da?* 1927

Eines Tages erkrankte eine Sängerin, die mit ihrem Schmalz die härtesten Seelen aufzuweichen verstanden hatte; wir standen vor einem wichtigen Personalwechsel. Am Ende war aber ein Ersatz gefunden, ein kleines, pusseliges, blondes Ding, das weinend erklärte, für einen Teller warmer Suppe jeden Abend drei Stunden lang in zwei Sprachen singen zu wollen. Diese Dame, aufgewachsen und erzogen an den literaturbesungenen Ufern des Genfer Sees, steht am Anfang einer Weltbewegung, sie trug zuerst den Namen Dada. Wir gaben ihn ihr in einer Stunde der Langeweile, zwischen kaltem Tee und Zigarettenstummel, niemand ahnte, was sich aus dieser gleichgültigsten aller Bezeichnungen gestalten würde.

Ich sehe sie immer noch vor mir, wie sie sich in ihrem oft gewendeten, abgeschabten Wollkleidchen vor dem anspruchsvollen Publikum, den betrunkenen Studenten, verbeugte. Es gab Unwürdige, die behaupteten, die Dame Dada stehe im Stimmbruch und man dürfe keine ernsthafte Kritik an ihre gesanglichen Leistungen legen.

Mademoiselle Dada war die Mistinguette des Kabarett Voltaire

Ein Dada-Wort: Jedermann sein eigener Fußball

Wieland Herzfelde, der Herausgeber der ersten deutschen Dada-Zeitschrift, die nach Aufhebung der Zensur erschien. Ihr damals verblüffender und unverständlicher Titel „Jedermann sein eigener Fußball" ist heute längst in den Sprachgebrauch übergegangen.

87

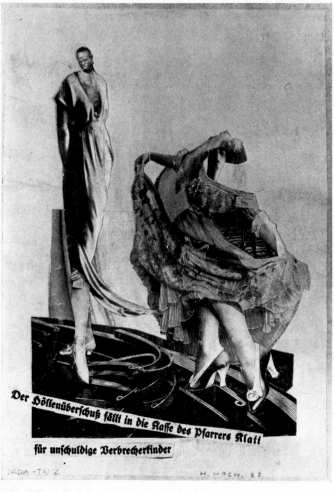

**Hannah Hoch** *Dada Dance* 1922 collage 12⅝ × 9 in.
Marlborough Fine Art (London) Ltd

and was engaged for exactly a year (between June 1919 and
June 1920) on a major and monumental sculpture-assemblage
and collage, which unfortunately has not survived, but which
according to reports would have ranked in scale and intensity with
Duchamp's *Large Glass* and Schwitters's massive assemblage, the
*Merzbau*.

**Hannah Hoch** *Bewacht* 1925 collage 10⅛ × 6¾ in.
Marlborough Fine Art (London) Ltd

Where Hausmann's *photomontages* are violent and somewhat strident, echoing his wildly anarchic temperament, those of Grosz are condensed and bitter, conveying the same savage flavour of social criticism that is evident, indeed paramount, in his drawings and paintings. Grosz's passionate hatred of the authoritarian, militaristic and bourgeois aspects of German society before

**Max Ernst** *Aquis submersus* 1919 oil on canvas 21¼ × 17¼ in.
Collection Sir Roland Penrose, London

**Kurt Schwitters** *NB* 1947 collage 13 × 10½ in.
Marlborough Fine Art (London) Ltd

**Johannes Baader** *The Author in his Home* about 1920 collage of pasted
photographs on book page 8½ × 5¾ in.
Museum of Modern Art, New York

**George Grosz** *The Engineer Heartfield* 1920 watercolour and collage
16½ × 12 in.
Museum of Modern Art, New York, gift of A.Conger Goodyear

**George Grosz** *Fit for Active Service* 1916–17 pen, brush and Indian ink
20 × 14¾ in.
Museum of Modern Art, New York, A. Conger Goodyear Fund

**George Grosz** *Metropolis* 1917 oil on cardboard 26¾ × 18¾ in.
Museum of Modern Art, New York

**George Grosz** *Republican Automatons* 1920 watercolour 23⅝ × 18⅝ in.
Museum of Modern Art, New York

**George Grosz** *In the Club* about 1922 pen and ink 7½ × 6 in.
Piccadilly Gallery, London

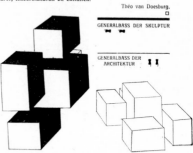

GENERALBASS DER SKULPTUR

GENERALBASS DER ARCHITEKTUR

*G.Material zur elementaren Gesaltung* 1923 page

and during the Weimar republic resulted in the production of some of the most bitingly satirical works of art ever created. Heartfield, also, was sustained by social anger, but his work, like his person, was more disciplined, sustained and polemical. Probably his most successful 'political' works date from the years after the decline of Dada. With great courage he lampooned the rebirth of Prussian militarism, of Hitler and the Nazis, until he was forced in 1933 into exile, first to Czechoslovakia, then to England.

Naturally, not all of the Dada activity in Berlin, particularly after the revolution was crushed in March 1919, was so consciously political as that of Heartfield or Grosz. Hans Richter, who had already made a considerable contribution in painting to the Zürich scene, on returning to Berlin in 1919 collaborated with the Swedish artist Viking Eggeling in exploring the rhythmical development of forms and colours, thinking about painting along lines analogous to music. In 1921 Richter, developing sequential ideas in painting in a further direction, completed his first abstract film, *Rythmus 21*, and in the same year Eggeling made his film *Diagonal Symphony*. Eggeling, who also had previously worked in Zürich, developed an all-embracing philosophy of

# Dada aisten gegen **Weimar**

LA

CABARET  zur  EL  PU  KAP  T ∫CH
NEBEN MIT BLAUEN  CHSTRASSE

Am Donnerstag, den 6. Februar 1919, abends 7½ Uhr, wird im Kaisersaal des Rheingold (Bellevuestraße) der

# OBERdADA

als

# Präsident des Erdballs

verkündigt werden nach dem Wort der Zeitung:

**?** „Wir werden in diesem Jahre wahrscheinlich noch einigemal wählen, den Prxsjdentrx, das V lkshaus. Und dann wollen wir uns nicht mehr bloß mit dem Instinkt, der mechanischen Zielsicherheit der unbewußt ainungsvollen Masse bescheiden, sondern das persönliche Genie s.ch.n gehən, das wir in irgend einer Schichte unseres Volkes endlich doch und doch hervorgebracht haben müssen, wenn w r nicht schon jetzt eine abgestorbene Rasse sein sollen!"

Zu dieser Suche werden alle geistigen und geistlichen Arbeiter, Volksbeauftragte, Bürger und Genossen beiderlei Geßchlechts (Soldaten ohne Rangabzeichen) erscheinen, denen an dem Glück der Menschheit gelegen ist.

Wir werden Weimar in die Luft sprengen. **Berlin** ist der Ort ¡ep ·· ep ·· Es wird niemand und nichts geschont werden.

Man erscheine in Massen!

## Der dadaistische Zentralrat der Weltrevolution.

BAAER, HAUSMANN, TRISTAN TZARA, GEORGE GROSZ, MARCEL JANCO, HANS ARP, RICHARD HÜLSENBECK, FRANZ ONnf, EUGEN ERNST, A. R. MEY**ER**

mphlet nominating Johannes Baader 'President of the Globe', Weimar 1919

harmony and basic design, foreshadowing later developments in the Bauhaus. This he called the 'Generalbass der Malerei' (the General—or common—Ground of Painting) and in it, in a similar way to that of Kandinsky, he attempted to 'orchestrate' the visual experience.

After 1919 the two Herzfeldes, Grosz and Jung, following their more programmed political bent, became engrossed in the left-wing publishing house Malik-Verlag. Baader and Hausmann then emerged as the central figures of a more typical Dadaist activity, generally hell-raising in the by now well-known Dada manner. Baader, for instance, appeared to have no inhibitions whatsoever; he was prone to continuous provocative gestures, to interrupting church services, and during the inauguration ceremony of the new German Republic at the Weimar State Theatre he cast from the balcony printed flysheets nominating himself not only the first President of the new state but also the President of the Globe.

Baader was a strange character, much older than the rest of the Dadaists, a natural anarchist who in his own obsessive way had been attacking and subverting organized society in a Dada manner long before the movement. His freedom from conventional restrictions or inhibitions was seized upon by the younger Dadaists as embodying both the destructive and the healing force of instinctive anarchism. Brandishing the titles he claimed for himself, Superdada, President of World Justice, Secret President of the League of Superdadist Intertelluric Nations, Representative of the Desks of Schoolmaster Hagendorff, formally architect and writer, he carried through the Germany of those years the banner of his individual and lyrical madness.

## Cologne—Ernst and the hallucinatory vision

Max Ernst was a different sort of personality. Coolly rational, he combined the talents for imaginative research with a mind that could embrace an almost gothic sense of fantasy, a mind that reversed the process of Baader's, rendering the organized into chaos, by being capable of facing the most extreme or bizarre image as if it were totally normal and expected. Ernst is generally considered as a Surrealist; but there is no essential difference in point of view, in content, or in style between his work before the

**Max Ernst** *Dadameter* drawing from *Die Schammade* 1920

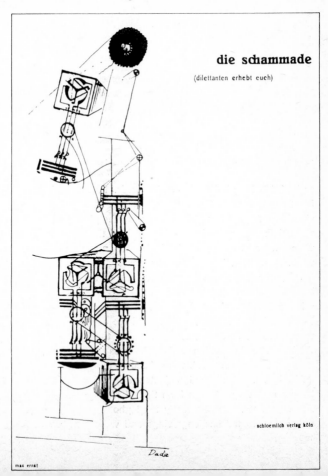

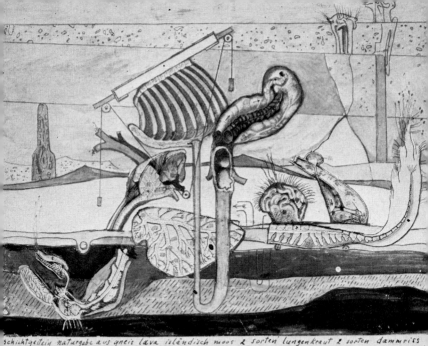

schichtgestein naturgabe aus gneis lava isländisch moos 2 sorten lungenkraut 2 sorten dammriss herzgewächse  b) dasselbe in fein poliertem kästchen etwas te

**Max Ernst** *Stratified Rocks* 1920 anatomical engraving altered with gouache and pencil 6 × 8⅜ in. Museum of Modern Art, New York

end of 1923 and that done afterwards. Everything that Max Ernst contributed to the Surrealist movement, and as far as the visual arts are concerned he was one of the pivotal figures, was more than merely implicit in his work of the Dada period, to which indeed belongs much of his best-known and significant work. Surrealism, 'proclaimed' by André Breton in 1924, grew directly out of Dada, and Ernst was one of the most important bridging personalities.

Ideas about the use of chance, automatism and the random configuration of images, which we have already noted in the work of Arp and others, were central to the painting of Ernst. We have already mentioned his techniques of *decalcomania* and *frottage*, but it is perhaps his use of collage that is most significant and original. His method of juxtaposing cut-outs and pasted images was very different from that of his colleagues in Berlin and elsewhere. First, he rarely used photographic images, but rather recombined line engravings and woodcuts. For him the collage had very little in common, either aesthetically or in terms of symbolic images, with those of the Cubists from whom the other Dada *colleurs* developed. It was the actual juxtaposition and confrontation of images that mattered, the discovery of a new figurative 'reality' brought about by the chance meeting of previously unrelated images—an idea that the later Surrealists were to take up as a central thesis. Ernst thought of the individual cut-out elements in terms of a new and irrational reality produced by the conjunction of images, '. . . the meeting of two distant realities on a plane foreign to them both', a process which produced a 'culture of systematic displacement and its effects'. Very few of his works could strictly be called collages, for the majority

**Max Ernst** *Let There Be Fashion, Down With Art* about 1919 from a set of 8 lithographs. Museum of Modern Art, New York

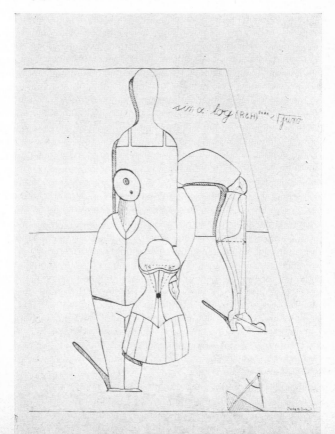

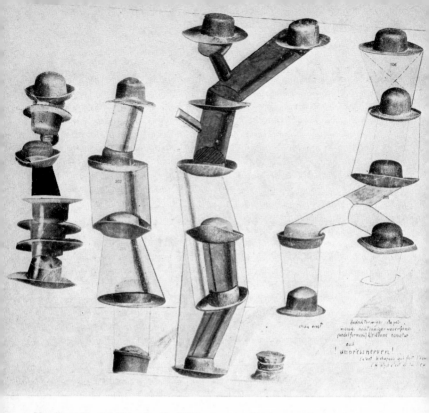

**Max Ernst** *The Hat Makes the Man* 1920 collage, pencil, ink, watercolour
14 × 18 in. Museum of Modern Art, New York

were printed images altered by painting and drawing upon them.
This technique, which of necessity was executed on a small scale,
was soon to be adapted to large paintings. The placing together
of previously unrelated images as it were created a springboard
from which could be discovered a further 'hallucinatory' level of
imagery, and this led to such paintings as *The Elephant Celebes*,
which, though clearly derived from collage in the juxtaposition of
disparate elements, were entirely painted, in an almost *trompe
l'oeil* manner. There is in these early paintings, which it must be
emphasized pre-date Surrealism proper by several years, the
narrative, illusionist and dream-like space that was to be later
explored by Dali, Magritte and others.

Max Ernst had made contact with Apollinaire and Arp before
the war, but, in his own words: 'On 1 August 1914 M.E. died.

He was resurrected on 11 November 1918 as a young man who aspired to find the myths of his time. Occasionally he consulted the eagle who brooded the egg of his prenatal life.' In 1919 he came across the paintings of De Chirico with their mysterious space and hallucinatory presence which sparked off his experiments in collage. These fall into two distinct families of images, the mechanical and the organic. The collages combine both 'hard' and 'soft' images, those of extraordinary machines made up from engineering illustrations and those of a biomorphic character resulting from the use of anatomical and biological engravings.

About the same time, with the writer and painter Johannes Baargeld, Ernst formed 'The Dada Conspiracy of the Rhineland'.

**Max Ernst** *Drawing* 1920 collage and drawing 7¼ × 5⅜ in. Anneley Juda Fine Art, London

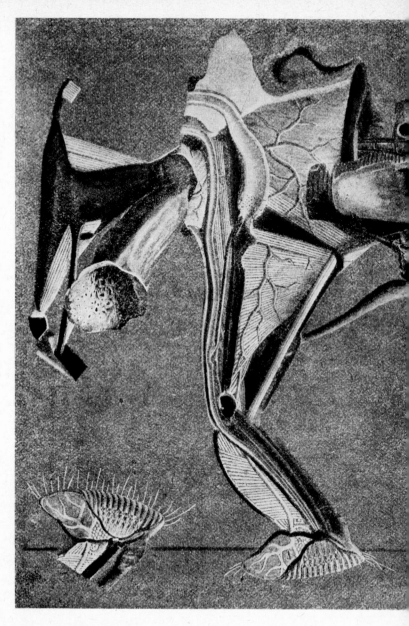

**Max Ernst** *The Horse, He's Sick* 1920 collage, pencil and ink $5\frac{3}{4} \times 8\frac{1}{2}$ in.
Museum of Modern Art, New York

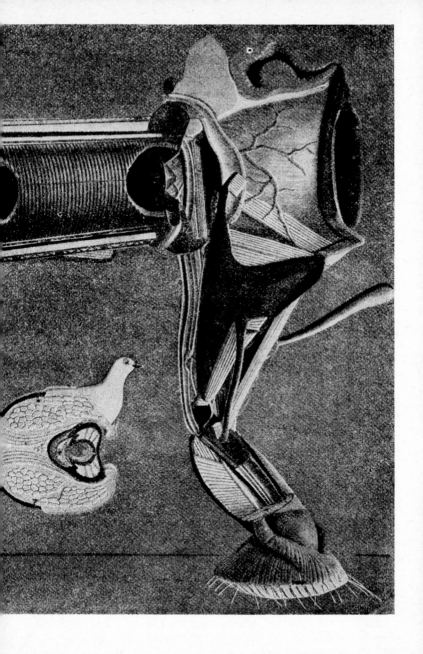

else lasker-schüler legte am 12. febr. 1920 däubler folgenden grabstein
in die nabelhöhle: vous qui passez priez pour cette dame qui en petant
par le cul rendit l'âme. der nabelmund däublers antwortete: ein reh? —
dein weh: — du hnnd.

der plumpe Roßtäuscher.

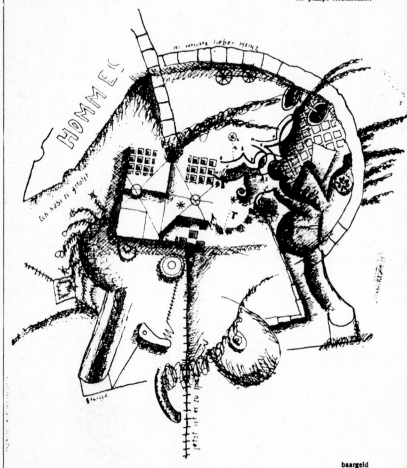

**Johannes Baargeld** *Dadameter* drawing from *Die Schammade* 1920

arp

**Hans Arp** *Dadameter* drawing from *Die Schammade* 1920

*On pages 114 and 115*
Catalogue of Cologne Dada Exhibition 1920 cover
Collection Timothy Baum, New York

ich bin nicht mehr in der Lage meinen sattel zu sättigen     baargeld

für dreigliede-
rung des dada-
istischen orga-
nismus

was die zeitungen mir vor-
werfen, ist unwahr. ich habe
noch niemals bauchdecken-
reflexe zur erhöhung der licht-
wirkung meiner bilder ver-
wendet. ich beschränke mich
lediglich auf rinozerisierte
rülpspinzetten.     max ernst

— besuchen Sie DADA?
— ich habe kein BEDÜRFNIS
— dada ist keine BEDÜRFNIS-
  ANSTALT.

jeder besucher dieser ausstellung ist prädestinierter dadaist entweder
lächelt er freimütig man kann ihn sodann als edeldadaist ansprechen
oder er fällt dem irrwahn des antidadaismus anheim zu spät bemerkt
er die personalunion von metzger und opferlamm in sich     er ist
dadaist schlechthin

כשר
חברה גמילות הסדים
חברה אהבת רעים
חברה הכנסת כלה
חברה גמילות הסדים
כשר על פסח

der wecker mit schluß für
erstgebärende
von Dr. Val. SERNER läuft
mit der geburt ab
                    baargeld

die liebe auf dem zweirad ist
die wahre nächstenliebe
                    baargeld

ich grüße nur noch simulanten

dadamax ernst

# DADA

## ausstellung

## DADA-VORFRÜHLING

**Gemälde**
**Skulpturen**
**Zeichnungen**
**Fluidoskeptrik**
**Vulgärdilettantismus**

die urne des dadaisten max ernst
erfreut sich außerordent-
licher beliebt- heit wiewohl
ich mir selber die größte
mühe —— —— gebe 
———————— baargeld ————————
(ich habe kein kissen für meine urne)

Baargeld was then publishing a magazine *Der Ventilator* which evinced strong Dadaistic and subversive tendencies together with an extreme left-wing political position. During its brief life this journal reached a wide audience, achieving a circulation of twenty thousand copies before it was closed down by the post-war British army of occupation. After joining Ernst, Baargeld found himself serving both politics and Dadaism; he founded the Communist Party of the Rhineland, but also painted and made collages in the Dada manner. Both he and Ernst believed it possible to keep the two activities separate, though complementary, and perhaps it is for this reason that their political militancy and the contents of their publications (*Der Ventilator* was succeeded by *Die Schammade*, an untranslatable neologism which Richter suggests might mean 'a serious charade') seem so much more sophisticated than many others.

Cologne, in some ways spiritually closer to Paris than to Berlin, demonstrated a certain cross-fertilization with Paris. *Die Schammade* also printed articles and poems by the French Dadaists Aragon, Breton, Eluard, Ribemont-Dessaignes and Soupault. Though Ernst and Baargeld were central to Cologne Dada, there was also another group which went under the rather endearing name of 'Stupid', consisting primarily of the painters Heinrich and Angelika Hoerle. But it was Ernst who was the moving personality behind a big exhibition, one of the most famous of all the provocative Dada manifestations, which was organized in April 1920. Baargeld and Ernst had for some time been in the habit of working together on the same picture; a process in which they were later joined by Hans Arp. These works, in which it was felt the process of collaboration 'liberated' irrational images, rather in the manner of a visual version of the party game of Consequences, were christened 'Fatagagas', which was short for the marvellously inconsequential title 'Fabrication des Tableaux Garantis Gazométriques'.

The 1920 exhibition consisted only of work by the three artists, some of them collaborations and others individual works. A great deal of planning went into the arrangement of the exhibition in order to produce the maximum amount of shock, scandal and social consternation. A site was found in the centre of the city, in a covered courtyard behind a café. The only entrance was through a public lavatory, and the audience unsuspectingly channelled through this route by the advance

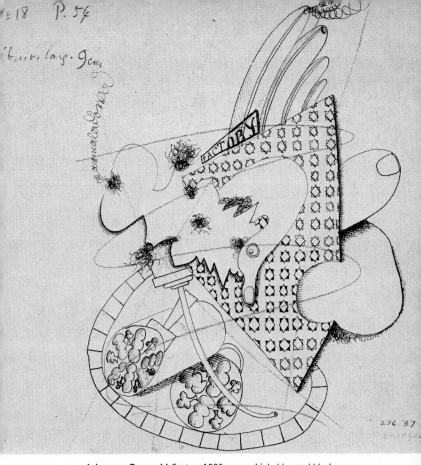

**Johannes Baargeld** *Factory* 1920 pen and ink, blue and black crayon
13¾ × 14¼ in. Museum of Modern Art, New York

publicity and the posters outside, was confronted by a room full of bizarre objects and incomprehensible drawings. That was not all, however, for the exhibition was opened by a young girl dressed as for her first communion who suddenly began to recite obscene verses. A similar violence appeared in the exhibits themselves: Baargeld exhibited a 'sculpture' consisting of an alarm clock and a head of woman's hair apparently drowned in an aquarium of blood, and Ernst produced, among other objects, a form carved in very hard wood to which an axe was attached by a chain, accompanied by a notice inviting those who wished to assist in destroying the sculpture.

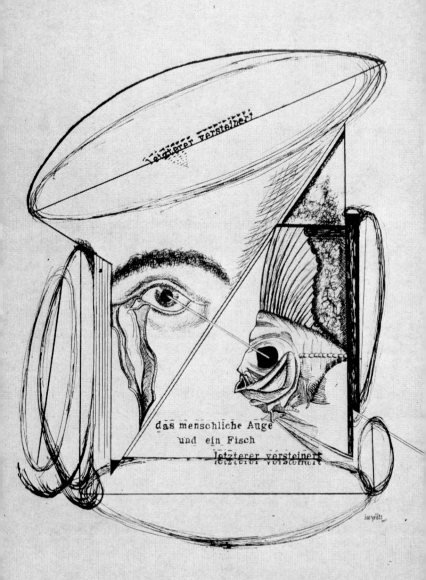

das menschliche Auge
und ein Fisch
letzterer versteinert

## Hanover—Schwitters, freedom through lyricism

In the work and in the mind of Kurt Schwitters there was little
violence. Rather, an overwhelming tenderness for everything that
exists. Schwitters was a visionary, almost a mystic, and most
certainly pro-art. Writing in 1920, he commented that there are
two sorts of Dadaists, the 'kernel' Dadaists and the 'husk'
Dadaists—a pun on the name of his Berlin opponent, for the
word 'Hüls' is German for 'husk': '. . . the husk Dadaists peeled
off from the original kernel under their leader Huelsenbeck, and
in so doing took part of the kernel with them.' Schwitters opposed the basic attitudes implicit in such comments of Huelsenbeck's as, 'All in all, art should get a good thrashing,' and 'Dada
is carrying on a kind of propaganda against art and against
culture.'

In 1917 Schwitters was painting well within the Expressionist
orbit, but within two years, and to a great extent independently—
although he must obviously have heard something of the furore
from Zürich and Berlin—he began in personal isolation to make
works 'composed of heterogeneous elements reunited in the work
of art by means of glue, hammer and nails, of paper, rags, bits of
machine, oil-paint, lace, etc.'. Not only 'everything the artist spits
is art', but for Schwitters everything the artist's eye fell upon was
potential art. He more than anyone else saw the aesthetic
potential of the unconsidered and the discarded.

José Pierre once called him, in a very telling phrase, 'the
archaeologist of the present'. Schwitters's attitude to the débris of
his contemporary urban society, to the printed ephemera, the
discarded papers and packages, the mass-media material, the
broken and abandoned machinery, the useless and the over-
looked, was shot through and through with an intense, private
and poetic vision. The discovered object itself contained its own
presence which guaranteed it to be a fit subject for art. In the last
resort he was a sort of realist, for the subject, the content of a work
of art as far as he was concerned, was finally the material itself
and the constituent parts of which the work was composed.

**Johannes Baargeld** *The Human Eye and a Fish, the Latter Petrified*
1920 pen and ink, pasted paper $12\frac{1}{4} \times 9\frac{3}{8}$ in.
Museum of Modern Art, New York

Schwitters's concept of 'Merz', itself a word 'discovered' from an accidental configuration in one of his collages, being found embedded in the phrase 'Kommerz und Privatbank', from a scrap of advertisement collaged into a work, is a concept of the artist's total response to his environment. There would seem to be no clear distinction here between what is art and what is not; at least in terms of more conventional ideas of the role of art. If Merz is art, then everything is art. The idea that the subject matter of art could be open, be conditioned merely by choice and chance, no longer required to be 'noble' or 'aesthetic', is of course central to most Dada thinking. But no one developed this principle so ruthlessly,

*Opposite*
**Kurt Schwitters** *Weltenkreise* 1919 assemblage and oil $46\frac{1}{8} \times 32\frac{5}{8}$ in. Marlborough Fine Art (London) Ltd

**Kurt Schwitters** *Drucksache* 1919 stamp drawing and collage with crayon $9 \times 7\frac{1}{2}$ in. Marlborough Fine Art (London) Ltd

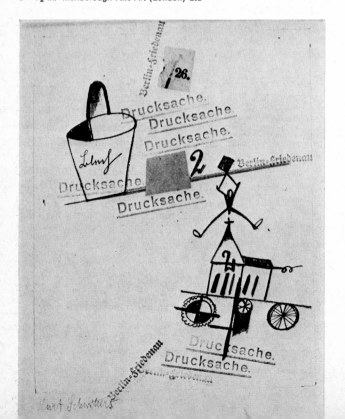

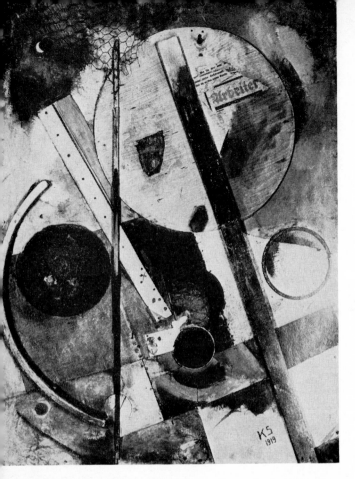

**Kurt Schwitters** *Das Arbeiterbild* 1919 assemblage and collage 49¼ × 36 in.
Moderna Museet, Stockholm

so logically, as Schwitters. For him the total environment was
potential art. The creative art consisted in regarding, in selecting,
in comparing and contrasting. Reality re-presented was reality
transformed and transcended.

He collected not only the visual débris of his environment,
piling up the junk like a jackdaw around his house in Hanover so
that the heaps of disparate objects, each piece waiting, as it were,
its turn, themselves formed spontaneous assembled sculptures,
but he also collected, catalogued and filed the aural débris

**Kurt Schwitters** *Das Kotsbild* 1920 collage 10⅝ × 7⅝ in.
Marlborough Fine Art (London) Ltd

around him. He would sometimes go for long journeys in trains
and trams, circling and recircling the city, listening to the conversation of people, the chatter and gossip of working-class
housewives, and to snatches of sentimental songs preferred
by servant girls. These overheard fragments were collaged, as it
were, verbally into his poems, one or two of which constitute the
most enduring literary works of the whole Dada period. Whether
writing in a fairly traditional idiom, as in the 'Anna Blume', whose
imagery, indeed verbal iconography, he constantly explored and

123

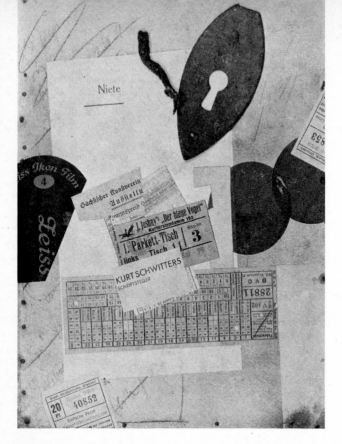

**Kurt Schwitters** *Schriftstellar* 1921–2 collage and assemblage 12¾ × 10 in.
Marlborough Fine Art (London) Ltd

**Kurt Schwitters** *Merz Konstruktion* 1921 painted wood, wire, paper
Philadelphia Museum of Art, A.E.Gallatin Collection

identified with, or developing, in the 'Ur-Sonate' and similar
poems, the most far-out form of abstract sound-poetry, his contribution was highly personal and extraordinarily intense.

Taking the concept of abstract poetry much further than Tzara
he 'orchestrated' the sounds with his own complex notations.
This process, as also the process of development in his plastic
work, became more condensed and more formalized over a
period of time. The 'Ur-Sonate', for instance, originally a purely
improvised event, developed in a more organized and more simple

manner, changing slightly at each of its many performances, until it reached its final shape in 1932 when Schwitters solidified it into notated form. It would seem from reports that the range of his vocal organs and his theatrical powers of projection were quite extraordinary. There are many stories emphasizing his ability to move a hostile audience into a genuine experience of a new art form; and a performance of, for instance, the famous poem 'W', in which he held up a large placard simply decorated with the capital letter, and wailed, groaned and ululated the consonant in a wild, barbaric and primitive music, often bludgeoned the originally sceptical audience into an attitude of grudging acceptance.

Schwitters was a brilliant propagandist for his own work and for the ideas implicit in Dada as well as in Merz. He was tirelessly active and creative. When he was not cutting and pasting paper, or nailing together wood and junk, or compiling and performing sound poems, he was travelling on one tour or another, launching manifestations, reading his verse, painting rather bad academic portraits and teaching drawing. Together with Van Doesburg he introduced Dada to Holland, instigating a hilarious trip through that country.

His best-known work, however, is one which has not survived, or rather has survived only partly in its third version. The *Merzbau* or the *Schwitters-Säule* (Schwitters's Column) was an ever-growing, developing, changing and mutating work of art, begun in 1920, and continued in one form or another until his death in 1948. The first 'total environment' assemblage was a living synthesis of a private vision, the formulation of one man's environment.

It began as a plaster sculpture, standing in a large room in the house he inherited from his family in Hanover. But this work was in a continual state of change and transformation. Not only a plastic presentation, it was also a statement about the inner world of irony and poetry as well as the outer appearance of visual art. Added to the forms and planes that gradually began to fill the room, there were also niches and pockets that 'belonged' to

**Kurt Schwitters** *Sonate* from *Mecano* 1923

# SONATE

Grim glim gnim bimbim
grim glim gnim bimbim
grim glim gnim bimbim
grim glim gnim bimbim
grim glim gnim bimbim
grim glim gnim bimbim
grim glim gnim bimbim
grim glim gnim bimbim
bum bimbim bam bimbim
bum bimbim bam bimbim
bum bimbim bam bimbim
bum bimbim bam bimbim
grim glim gnim bimbim
grim glim gnim bimbim
grim glim gnim bimbim

grim glim gnim bimbim
bum bimbim bam bimbim
bum bimbim bam bimbim
bum bimbim bam bimbim
bum bimbim bam bimbim
Tila lola lula lola
tila lula lola lula
tila lola lula lola
tila lula lola lula
Grim glim gnim bimbim
grim glim gnim bimbim
grim glim gnim bimbim
grim glim gnim bimbim
bem bem
bem bem
bem bem
bem bem

Tata tata tui E tui E
tata tata tui E tui E
tata tata tui E tui E
tata tata tui E tui E
Tillalala tillalala
tillalala tillalala.
Tata tata tui E tui E
tata tata tui E tui E.
Tillalala tillalala
tillalala tillalala.
Tui tui tui tui tui tui tui tui
te te te te te te te te
tui tui tui tui tui tui tui tui
te te te te te te te te.
Tata tata tui E tui E
tata tata tui E tui E.
Tillalala Tilla lala
tillalala tilla lala

Tui tui . tui tui tui tui tui tui
te te te te te te te te
tui tui tui tui tui tui tui tui
te te te te te te te te
O be o be o be o be
o be o be o be o be.

KURT SCHWITTERS

*Mecano* 1923 cover

specific people: to Mondrian, to Arp, to Gabo, to El Lissitzky, to Malevich, to Mies, to Richter, to Van Doesburg, to the different members of his family. Each of these holes was like a reliquary for its 'owner', containing various objects—here a lock of hair, there a cigarette stub. There were toe-nail clippings and false teeth, a shoelace, a pen; there were letters and papers and all sorts of bizarre and inconsequential objects. There was even a bottle of urine with the donor's name on the label.

The reliquaries were continually shifting and changing. As the 'column' grew, some were sealed up and left deep inside; meanwhile new ones were opened up. Soon the *Merzbau* entirely filled the room. Schwitters could no longer move around it to work, and it was beginning to invade his own living space. He had one solution as the landlord of the house. Giving notice

**Van Doesburg, Huszar, Schwitters** poster for Dada performance in Holland 1923

to the tenants of the flat above, he knocked out the ceiling, and allowed the growing 'column' the freedom to spread itself along the upper floor.

It was his major work, and he regarded it as such. Of course it was never finished. It never could have been finished : even under ideal circumstances it would only be finished when it ceased to grow, and it would essentially only have done that upon his death. But it ceased to grow for another reason, for politics forced him to abandon it. He was obliged to flee from the Nazi régime to Norway, where he settled for four years. He began another 'column' in a building idyllically situated on an island in a fjord near Molde. But his flight north was not to provide a refuge after all, and he was forced to move again just ahead of the invading German armies. Doubly exiled, he arrived in England in 1940, and was immediately placed in an internment camp on the Isle of Man for seventeen months. After his release he lived with his son Ernst in London until the war ended in 1945. After this, he went to the Lake District where he was to live for the rest of his life.

It was here, in a barn at Ambleside, that Schwitters began his last *Merzbau*, the only one to marginally survive. The original Hanover one was destroyed by Allied bombs in an air-raid in 1943, and the Norwegian one was lost in a fire in 1951. In 1965 the Fine Art department of the University of Newcastle removed the deteriorating fragment of the Ambleside *Merzbau* to safer premises. The one completed wall with its subtle complex of images testifies to the artist's continuing vitality and creative imagination. Stylistically Schwitters, the most dedicated 'artist' among the Dadaists, responded like a delicate aesthetic barometer to the changing climate of the times without abandoning any of his own very personal characteristics. The comparison of the various *Merzbaue* gives an eloquent witness to this. From the photographs of the original Hanover work, we note a predominant constructivist flavour, it is in the spirit of De Stijl and specifically of Van Doesburg, while the Ambleside wall with its rough texture and subtle but muted colouring anticipates 'matter' painting, foreshadowing the work of such artists as Tapies and Burri in the fifties.

**Kurt Schwitters** *Merzbau* Hanover 1920–36

*On pages 132 and 133*
**Kurt Schwitters** *Merzbau* Ambleside 1945–8
Department of Fine Art, University of Newcastle upon Tyne

## Paris—last fling and obsequies

It was in Paris that the flow of Dada finally dissipated itself in rather incestuous squabbles; and was ultimately to be transformed under the impact of French rationality into Surrealism.

In its Parisian aspect, Dada did not demonstrate as specific and defined a quality as it did, for instance, in Berlin. Unlike the German approach, political attitudes played little or no part, and unlike the Zürich spirit, attempts at free-wheeling anarchism—despite provocative efforts by Tzara, and in the early days by

At the Max Ernst exhibition Paris 1920
Left to right: René Hilsum, Benjamin Péret, Serge Charchoune, Philippe Soupault, Jacques Rigaut (upside down), André Breton

Francis PICABIA.

## Carnet du Docteur Aisen

Marcel Boulenger est toujours le surnuméraire de Sainte-Geneviève.

H.-L. Lenormand (neurologue) est atteint de sagesse précoce.

Metzinger est un joli rossignol mécanique.

Le cubisme est-il un art espagnol ou français ? répondre au '' Sans Pareil ''.

Tristan Tzara s'est cassé une côte, trop pressé d'aller voir Houdini. A la sortie du spectacle il m'a affirmé être le seul homme qui ne soit pas pédéraste—

Ribemont-Dessaignes dit '' l'autre '', a été malade de rire en lisant le dernier article de Pinturrichio dans le Carnet.

Edgar Varèse fait du cinéma. Il tourne actuellement un film dada.

**Francis Picabia** *Tableau Dada* from *Cannibale* 1920

SZEGEDIN

Silence RD.

**Georges Ribemont-Dessaignes** *Silence* about 1915 oil on canvas
36¼ × 28⅞ in. Museum of Modern Art, New York, Katherine S. Dreiser Bequest

Breton—were by and large confused riots or damp squibs. The
climate of Paris, with the background of Rimbaud, Jarry and
Apollinaire, was essentially literary, and being so was perhaps in
the last issue too much involved in verbalization to reflect the
nihilistic and inconsequent standpoints taken up elsewhere.
Predictably, it was the French, and specifically André Breton, who

*391* (1917–24) page

imposed a concrete philosophical system upon the open-ended assumptions of Dada, and who defined its techniques concerned with chance, automatism and the irrational into an orthodox Freudian and Marxist viewpoint, incorporating the anarchic individualism into a rigid and structural theory.

However, in 1919 the coming of Tristan Tzara was awaited by a

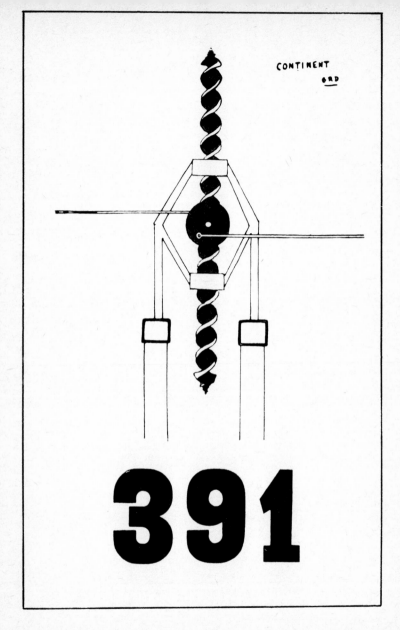

*391* (1917–24) cover

**Gino Severini** *Le Nord-Sud* 1912 drawing 21¾ × 16½ in.
Grosvenor Gallery, London

# SALLE GAVEAU
### 45-47, Rue la Boëtie

# FESTIVAL DADA

**Mercredi 26 Mai 1920 à 3 h. après-midi**

PROGRAMME :

Tous les Dadas se feront tondre les cheveux
sur la scène !

1. le sexe de dada
2. pugilat sans douleur par Paul DERMÉE
   le célèbre illusionniste Philippe SOUPAULT
   manière forte par Paul ELUARD
   le nombril interlope musique de Georges RIBEMONT-DESSAIGNES
   Interprété par Mlle Marguerite BUFFET
   festival manifeste presbyte par Francis PICABIA
   Interprété par André BRETON et Henri HOURY
   corridor par le Docteur SERNER
   le rastaquouère André BRETON
   vaste opéra par Paul DRAU...
   la deuxième aventure de
   monsieur Aa l'antipyrine par Tristan TZARA

Personnages : Absorbtion ........ Paul ELUARD
Oreille ........... André BRETON
Mme Interruption .... Mlle Marguerite BUFFET
Le cerveau désinteressé .. G. RIBEMONT-DESSAIGNES
M. Saturne ........ Théodore FRAENKEL
M. Aa ...........

11. vous m'oublierez sketch par André BRETON et Philippe SOUPAULT

12. la nourrice américaine par Francis PICABIA
    Musique sodomiste interprétée par Marguerite BUFFET

13. manifeste baccarat par Georges RIBEMONT-DESSAIGNES

Gauche ....... Georges BRETON
Droite ....... Georges RIBEMONT-DESSAIGNES
Milieu ....... Tristan TZARA
M. Oxigène ..... Philippe SOUPAULT

14. jeu d'échecs par Céline ARNAULD
    danse frontière par Georges RIBEMONT-DESSAIGNES

16. système DD par Louis ARAGON

17. puits des javanais par Francis PICABIA

18. poids public par Paul ELUARD

M. ELUARD
Mme ELUARD
FRANCIS PICABIA LE PIRE

19. vaseline symphonique par Tristan TZARA
    Jouée par 20 personnes

Chacun de vous a dans le cœur un coupable
une montre et un petit paquet de merde.

Dada est le bonheur à la coque

small, but extremely articulate group as a sort of messianic visitation. Picabia was publishing his magazine *391*, while other pre-Dada reviews such as *Nord-Sud, Sic,* and Breton's own *Littérature* were circulating in artistic circles, backed up by Duchamp's importation of his two reviews *Rongwrong* and *The Blind Man*. *Littérature*, before the appearance of Tzara on the scene, seemed firmly ensconced in pre-war attitudes, despite contributions by Philippe Soupault, Louis Aragon, Paul Eluard, and of course Breton himself, all of whom had contributed in one way or another to the original Zürich issues of *Dada*. Though *Littérature* mounted the famous questionnaire 'Why do you write?', which resulted in many ironic and inconsequential replies, the tone of the magazine was largely set by articles and poems by an older generation of writers such as André Gide, Paul Valéry, Max Jacob and Blaise Cendrars.

Tzara's intention was to place himself firmly at the head of Parisian Dada, and his original impact was considerable. His arrival was quickly followed by a violent but confused series of 'provocations', including one on the twenty-fifth anniversary of the riot which broke out at the première of Jarry's *Ubu Roi*. This series was climaxed in May 1921 by a large gathering at the Salle Gaveau, where the audience, entering completely into the spirit of nihilism, armed themselves with tomatoes, eggs and bits of meat to hurl at the stage.

At this point the movement had split into three groups led respectively by Tzara, Picabia and Breton, each alliance taking up a position of increasing antagonism towards the others. Everything came to a head with an event which seemed less to provoke the public than to shake the movement to pieces, the 'Barrès Trial'.

The writer Maurice Barrès had been a hero of the Dadaists and many of them felt strongly about his later betrayal of their cause in writing for the reactionary newspaper *L'Echo de Paris.* The 'Barrès Trial' where he was 'indicted and tried by Dada', was a farce but for the Breton faction none the less solemn. Wearing mock-judicial gear, Breton acted as President of the Tribunal and Ribemont-Dessaignes as Public Prosecutor, while the Accused was represented by a tailor's dummy. Benjamin Péret testified as the Unknown Soldier and Aragon as Counsel for the Defence

Poster for Dada Festival at the Salle Gaveau 1920

# RONGWRONG

Greetings.

SIRIO MATCH CO. BROOKLYN, N. Y.

*Littérature* 1922 cover

*Opposite*
**Marcel Duchamp** *Rongwrong* 1917 cover
Collection Timothy Baum, New York

asked for the death of his client. Breton in summing up stated that a man who renounces 'that which is unique in himself' and who 'interferes in whatever revolutionary power may reside in the activity of those who might be tempted to learn from his first lesson' is guilty of 'offences against the security of the spirit'. Here we have evidence of Breton's essential seriousness, to which Tzara objected on principle. Tzara himself was meanwhile clowning in the traditional Dada fashion. With his cerebral approach, Breton had grown tired of 'provocations', besides which he felt that Dada had already broken down the old attitudes and

143

# Portrait de TRISTAN TZARA
### par
## FRANCIS PICABIA

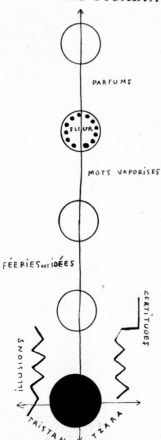

**Francis Picabia** Portrait of Tristan Tzara from *Cannibale* 1920

concepts, and now it was time to act constructively and build on the wreckage of shattered bourgeois values.

Picabia left the trial before it ended and shortly afterwards publicly withdrew from Dada, stating that '. . . the Dada spirit really existed only between 1913 and 1918, the period in which

# FRANCIS PICABIA

EST UN IMBÉCILE, UN IDIOT, UN PICKPOCKET !!!

**MAIS**

IL A SAUVÉ ARP DE LA CONSTIPATION !

LA PREMIÈRE ŒUVRE MÉCANIQUE A ÉTÉ CRÉÉE PAR MADAME TZARA LE JOUR OÙ ELLE MIT AU MONDE LE PETIT TRISTAN, ET POURTANT ELLE NE CONNAISSAIT PAS

## FUNNY-GUY

# FRANCIS PICABIA

est un professeur espagnol imbécile, qui n'a jamais été dada   FRANCIS PICABIA N'EST RIEN !

# FRANCIS PICABIA AIME LA MORALE DES IDIOTS

LE BINOCLE DE ARP EST UN TESTICULE DE TRISTAN

# FRANCIS PICABIA N'EST RIEN !!!!

**FRANCIS PICABIA**

EST UN LOUSTIC
EST UN IDIOT
EST UN CLOWN
N'EST PAS UN PEINTRE
N'EST PAS UN LITTÉRATEUR
EST UN IMBÉCILE
EST UN ESPAGNOL
EST UN PROFESSEUR
N'EST PAS SÉRIEUX
EST RICHE
EST PAUVRE

MAIS : ARP ÉTAIT DADA AVANT DADA

BINET-VALMER AUSSI
RIBEMONT-DESSAIGNES AUSSI
PHILIPPE SOUPAULT AUSSI
TRISTAN TZARA AUSSI
MARCEL DUCHAMP AUSSI
THÉODORE FRAENKEL AUSSI
LOUIS VAUXCELLES AUSSI
FRANTZ JOURDAIN AUSSI
LOUIS ARAGON AUSSI
PICASSO AUSSI
DERAIN AUSSI
MATISSE AUSSI
MAX JACOB AUSSI
ETC... ETC... ETC.....

EXCEPTÉ FRANCIS PICABIA !

LE SEUL ARTISTE COMPLET !

# FRANCIS PICABIA VOUS CONSEILLE D'ALLER VOIR SES TABLEAUX AU SALON D'AUTOMNE,

ET VOUS PRÉSENTE SES DOIGTS A BAISER.

**FUNNY-GUY.**

Les hommes couverts de croix font penser à un cimetière

Si vous voulez avoir les idées propres changez-en comme de chemises

---

Francis Picabia *Funny Guy* 1921 handbill

*Dadaphone* 1920 cover
Collection Timothy Baum, New York

it never really stopped evolving and transforming itself; after that it became as uninteresting as the output of the Ecole des Beaux Arts . . . in the desire to prolong its life, Dada has shut itself up within itself'. Soon Breton was to write in a new issue of *Littérature,* at a time when he was already forming his ideas which were later to be announced in the 'First Surrealist Manifesto' of 1924, 'Dadaism cannot be said to have served any other purpose than to keep us in the perfect state of availability in which we are at present, and from which we shall now in all lucidity depart towards that which now calls us.'

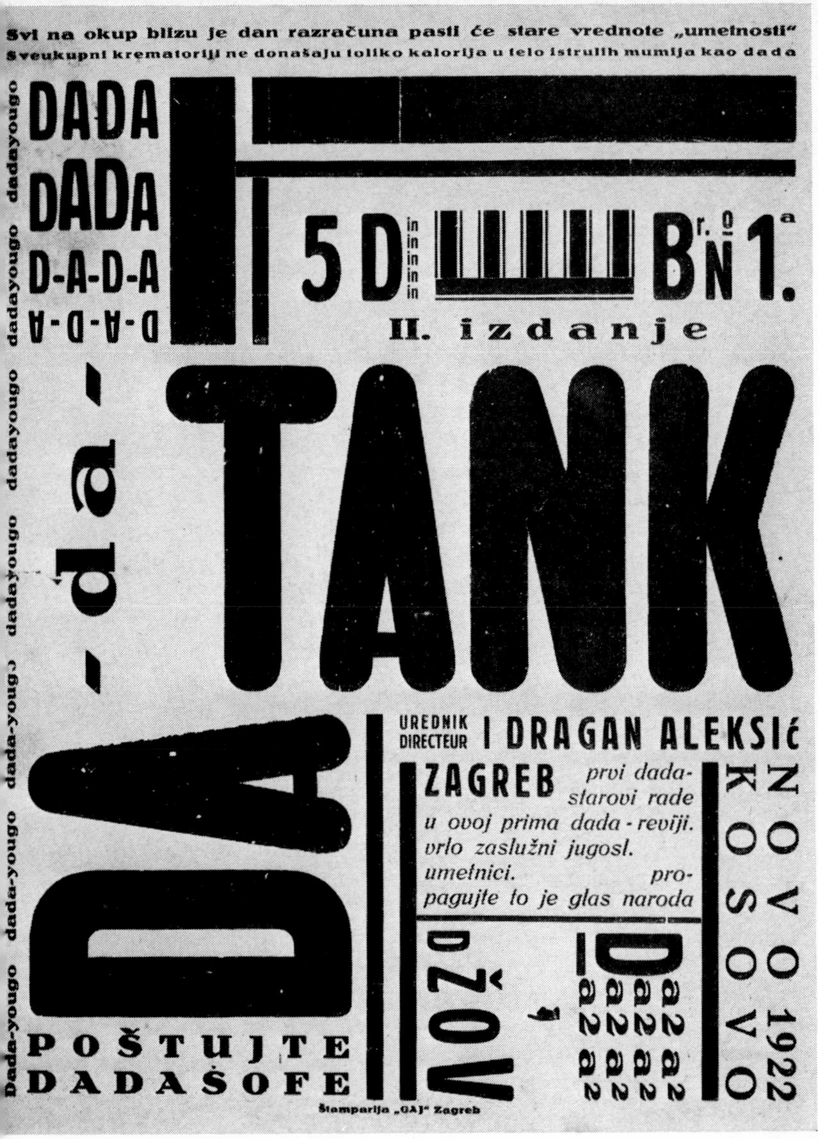


*Dada-Tank* 1922 cover
Collection Timothy Baum, New York

## Dada is dead—long live Dada

Dada was formally interred and obsequies pronounced by Doesburg, Arp, Richter, Schwitters and Tzara, when these artists met in Weimar in May 1922 at the 'Bauhausfest'. Tzara delivered a funeral oration which was later repeated in Jena and Hanover. Elsewhere Dada survived a few more years. In Barcelona the influence of Picabia survived; a group surrounding the magazine *Tank* in Zagreb, Yugoslavia, was very active during the early twenties, and there was a sort of Indian summer in Hungary, first with the magazine *Ma* edited by Lajos Kassak, then, in 1927, with the group 'Green Donkey' under the provocative leadership of Odon Palasowski.

Though Dada was dead as a movement it still continued underground, as it were, as an individual attitude, as private creative activity, in the work primarily of Duchamp and Picabia, in the photographs and objects of Man Ray, in the films of Richter and Viking Eggeling. 'Dada will survive only by ceasing to exist,' J. E. Blosche had written as early as 1919 in his manifesto 'Dada Prophetie'. As a public manifestation it 'ceased to exist' after the early twenties because the social climate was no longer conducive to its questioning and anarchist spirit. Yet sooner or later a new configuration of social and political conditions would be bound to come about that would provide the mental climate for its revival.

This is exactly what happened during the middle fifties. The Korean War, the Bomb, and probably more than anything else Khruschev's revelations at the 20th Party Congress in 1956, which sparked off the New Left, provided analogies with Weimar and the 1917 revolution. Young artists in New York, Paris and Milan independently rediscovered the forty-year-old texts of Zürich and Berlin, rediscovered the principles of chance, of ironic and anarchistic detachment, and adapted them to their own circumstances and changed conditions. Under the blanket titles of Neo-Dada in America and New Realism on the continent, Dada surfaced once more in a different guise, bearing new banners. Surviving as an individual ethic, particularly in the person of Duchamp, the 'state of mind' consistently held by a few individuals becomes again one held by the group and applicable to the immediate social environment.

Neo-Dada is of course different, even in some fundamentals. The movement of the late fifties and early sixties was mainly centred on the fine arts, though there has also been a distinct resurgence in concrete poetry and music during the last fifteen years. We have noted that Dada moved into Surrealism, an idiom that ultimately found its most profound expression on the visual plane, and one may also note a sort of reversal of this process. Surrealist concepts such as the use of automatism were central to the New York Abstract Expressionists and to the Parisian Tachists. Nowhere is this more evident than in the work of Jackson Pollock, whose development was consistent from his early Surrealist mode inspired by André Masson to the unique imagery of his mature style.

In America, with the developing New York School, and the increasing awareness of an indigenous culture and an art that was for the first time truly American and free from the shackles of the Ecole de Paris, the conditions were right for the appearance of a 'bohemia' and the attendant anarchist and anti-bourgeois gestures.

One of the key American figures behind this development was the composer John Cage. Much influenced by Edgard Varèse and Luigi Russolo and trained by Schönberg, he was the first musician to consistently explore elements of chance, and created the idiom now widely followed by many younger composers. Working with sound, he aimed at a sort of aleatory realism, a realism of the accidental. He saw music as something that was continually present, permanently in a flux with other aspects of perceptual experience, coming finally to regard it as part of a total experience and therefore as some sort of 'theatre'. 'Theatre,' he has stated, 'takes place all the time wherever one is, and art simply facilitates persuading one that this is the case.'

Here his ideas were very close to those of the painter Robert Rauschenberg, who, in his early field paintings of 1952, saw the canvas as a sort of recording device, which reflected the environment rather than depicting it, as a work in a state of permanent creation resulting from events taking place outside the picture. 'Painting relates to both art and life. Neither can be made. I try to act in the gap between the two.' He also wanted to step back into some sort of anonymity in the fact of the picture itself, an anonymity similar to the ironic detachment of Duchamp. He speaks of a *collaboration* with his materials. 'I don't want a painting to be an

149

**Robert Rauschenberg** *Canyon* 1959 combine painting 86½ × 23 in.
Collection Ileana Sonnabend

Robert Rauschenberg *Monogram* 1959 construction 48 × 72 × 72 in.
Moderna Museet Stockholm

expression of my personality . . . I'd really like to think that the artist could be just another kind of material in the picture . . . I don't want a picture to look like something it isn't. I want it to look like something it is. And I think a picture is more like the real world when it is made of the real world.'

Rauschenberg met John Cage when they were both working with the choreographer and innovator of the modern dance Merce Cunningham. This collaboration led to a series of theatre pieces dependent upon chance and random events performed during 1953 and 1954. The term 'Happening' had not at that time been invented, this was not to come until 1958 when circumstances brought together an extremly talented group of young people who attended Cage's classes at the New School for

Social Research in New York. Al Hansen, Dick Higgins and Allen Kaprow were outstanding members of this group, and under the influence of Cage's thinking, and together with such friends as the painters George Segal, Jim Dine, Claes Oldenburg and Larry Poons, they developed the idea of the 'collage event' in various directions, exploring audience participation and total theatre.

In many ways their ideas were influenced, if perhaps unconsciously, by the thinking of Existentialism. It is clear, particularly from the statements of Cage and Rauschenberg, that a body of work was developing that 'accords primacy to *existence*' rather than to essence. Following Rauschenberg, and to a lesser extent Jasper Johns, Neo-Dada 'event' art and assemblage, 'junk' sculpture and collage, became a dominant area of art activity in America. Of course, New York did not hold a monopoly for this development—indeed the European Dada revival pre-dated it. A group of artists banding together under the title 'Cobra', consisting of painters from Copenhagen, Brussels and Amsterdam, and led by Asger Jorn, mounted some events during the late

**Al Hansen** Programmed accidental sight and sound assemblage 1958–9
Reuben Gallery, New York

forties, while the Situationist and Léttriste groups (the latter concerned with concrete poetry) also mounted early proto-Happenings during the first years of the fifties.

However, it was about the same time as New York, or even shortly after, that the Paris- and Milan-based movement, known as 'New Realism' got under way. The outstanding figures were the Parisians Yves Klein and Jean Tinguely and the Milanese Piero Manzoni. The first of these, despite his apparently theatrical stunts which achieved wide publicity, like covering nude models in blue oil paint then rolling them across a canvas, was a profoundly serious thinker whose ideas have been of enormous influence, and his act of making a picture by strapping a canvas with the priming still wet to the roof-rack of his car and driving from Paris to the Riviera, in order to get an imprint of the landscape conditioned by rain, wind and weather, was related to the ideas of Rauschenberg and the logical outcome of certain philosophical implications of the time.

Tinguely also wanted to 'make things that are so close to life that they exist as simply and as changeably and permanently as a cat jumping, or a child playing, or a truck going by outside . . . Life *is* play, movement, continual change.' It is from such a point of view that Tinguely constructs his extraordinary machines which comment upon the 'absurdity' of our relationship with the objective world, and which with their built-in programme of self-destruction provide a sort of social comment on the 'absurdity' of our behaviour and pretensions.

Piero Manzoni was perhaps more in the classical spirit of Dada, and during his brief working life created innumerable objects which embodied an extraordinary and savage irony. With concepts like his 'line', a series of enormously long drawings consisting of single continuous lines on separate rolls of paper, all of which when added together form the circumference of the world, and his enigmatic *boîtes de merde*, created individual works, each of which was a logically self-contained concept. With his piercing intelligence and his ruthlessly single-minded approach, he is the successor who has approached nearest to the ideal of detachment set up by Duchamp.

In England, also, works in a reformed Dada spirit were produced during the second half of the fifties. William Green made paintings by riding a bicycle across his canvases. John Latham was very early on the scene with his assemblages of books known

**Piero Manzoni** *White on White* 1962–3 mixed media $31\frac{1}{2} \times 23\frac{5}{8}$ in.
Galleria dell' Obelisco, Rome

as *Noit* and his use of fire as an element of the work in the *Skoob Towers*. While Gustav Metzger, whose concern is with time, change, decay and movement, was the first artist to use the phrase 'auto-destructive' art. Through the idiom of plastic structures which disintegrate under the influence of acids and other chemicals he comments upon the idea of permanence.

Neo-Dada, despite clear similarities and a distinct linear descent down a sort of family tree, has taken a fundamentally different colouring. The nihilism of Dada has given way to lyrical and poetic ambiguities, social anarchism has been replaced by social comment, and ironic paradox has been replaced by philosophical paradox. Claes Oldenburg, Jim Dine, Andy Warhol and Edward Kienholz have incorporated Dada elements to make comments upon the consumer society. Daniel Spoerri in France, with his concepts of an 'anecdoted topography of chance' and his 'snare pictures', where he traps the ephemeral, comments on the nature of permanence, the Happenings of the German artist Wolf Vostell are almost political in their allusions to violence, while those of the Parisian Jean-Jacques Lebel explore territory close to the Theatre of Cruelty, but with the same sort of consciousness of revolt and the new awareness of youth that made May 1968 possible. The German 'Zero' Group, Heinz Mack, Gunther Uecker and Otto Piene explore the nature of phenomena, causing the art-work to reflect natural and chance effects, arriving at a sort of Dada crossed with Constructivism, as does also the related Dutch group 'NUL' including Henk Peeters and Jan Schoonhoven. The English artist Patrick Hughes examines aspects of the nature of reality and perception, of paradox and ambiguity, operating in a territory that lies somewhere between Duchamp and René Magritte.

All of these last mentioned artists have been active for a decade or more. And younger artists are continually appearing on the scene with related preoccupations. The so-called 'Earth Art', with all its other titles such as Concept Art or Arte Povera, a style which has not yet jelled into one heading, is the most recent aspect of a post-Dadaistic approach. The artists concerned are in obvious opposition to form itself. There is an emotional involvement that

*On pages 156 and 157*
**Patrick Hughes** *Infinity Rock* 1968 ceramic, wood and sand
$14 \times 11 \times 14\frac{1}{2}$ in.
Collection the author

accepts the accidental configuration of *objets trouvés*, the use of mundane materials even more unstable than those used earlier by the 'junk' sculptors—the earth itself, the place where we live, is considered both as a medium and a working place. Many of the works are projects executed in isolated places, such as mile-long trenches dug in the desert. The art-work is itself not exhibited, the object presented being a dossier of plans and blueprints, photographs and geological samples. The point of the aesthetic idea lies in the concept. Where the Minimal is stripped of ideas, the Conceptual is almost nothing *but* ideas.

Dada was not simply an art-historical moment; it was, and is, a frame of mind, one that evolves to the changing conditions of society. Rather than being a series of events that took place between 1912 and 1923 it is a fluctuating point of view that has assumed a more and more central role in the aesthetic awareness of our culture. There is hardly an aspect of the mainstream fine arts today that has not been influenced by Dada. Even in Post-Constructivism and Minimal Art great emphasis is laid on spectator participation and the environmental aspect of the work. Schwitters's *Merzbau* in its final constructivist appearance, its use of random elements, and its scale *vis-à-vis* the spectator, was the great proto-environmental sculpture, echoed in many a Minimal work, in many a 'situation'.

In the work of three young artists at present beginning to build a reputation in London (taken at random, and one could find equivalent artists of the same generation in any art centre of the world), the lurking presence of Dada is unmistakable. These three artists exhibited together in London during 1969. Peter Joseph's contribution was approaching the Minimal, but it was constructed temporarily inside the exhibition space and was considered as an ephemeral 'event'. It was a vast yellow wall of stretched canvas, slightly wedge-shaped and just over eye-level in height. Its enormous size was a determining factor. Seventy-five feet in length, it ran completely down the centre of the largest of the exhibition rooms. The experience of standing beside it or walking slowly along its length was oddly disturbing; the enormous area of meticulously painted colour achieved a sort of super-saturation of pigment. The colour radiated from the object, and seemed almost to penetrate every cubic inch of the enclosed space. As a result of retinal fatigue, curious complementary colour effects could be noticed on the 'wall' surface, and its finely constructed straight edges would appear to waver and flicker in a disconcerting manner. The aesthetic experience lay altogether in the phenomenological aspect, the confrontation between spectator and object. This assumption stems from Dada ideas about the nature of the object, and it must be remembered that Duchamp was among the first to experiment with Optical effects in art.

The work of Timothy Drever was much more participatory in nature. In a darkened room painted entirely black, one discovered on the floor a series of shapes derived from logically consistent geometric sections of circular arcs drawn in a basic square module. These forms, flat sheets of wood, were painted black on one surface and white on the other, in such a manner that when the black side was uppermost the form vanished. The public were encouraged to rearrange the elements themselves into different

**Peter Joseph** *Yellow Wall* 1969 canvas on wood frame 75 × 6 ft
Exhibited Camden Arts Centre, London, 1969

**Timothy Drever** *Moonfield* 1969 hardboard shapes
Exhibited Camden Arts Centre, London, 1969

configurations, rendering them visible or invisible at will. Both of these artists have collaborated in environmental experiences in public places, integrating within the work the physical participation of the public and the casual passer-by.

Ed Herring's work is much more conceptual and is extremely sophisticated in basic plan. At the exhibition he shared with his two colleagues he constructed in the garden outside the gallery a rainwater catchment area which led water through pipes past a series of linked and glass-topped boxes set flush into the ground. Each of some twenty-odd boxes set down an incline contained different chemicals which in reaction to the rainwater gradually changed colour from white to various shades of red, blue and green, making a sort of chromatic meteorological imprint of the changing weather conditions. Herring has experimented widely in this area of experience, arranging objects in isolated parts of the countryside in such a manner that they define space, but also mutate and change to the dictates of time and the elements.

The work of art is more and more being thought of as an event, a situation, a direct confrontation with society. And it was just these values which were the central innovation of Zürich, New York and Berlin fifty-five years ago. 'Dada will survive only by ceasing to exist.' And so it has.

Ed Herring *Chemical System* 1969 within an outdoor area 104 × 66 ft
Exhibited Camden Arts Centre, London, 1969

# LITS

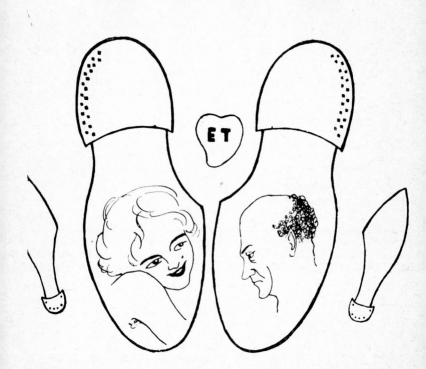

# RATURES

## Book List

Barr, Alfred H. (editor) *Fantastic Art, Dada, Surrealism* Museum of Modern Art, New York, 1947

Hugnet, Georges *L'Aventure Dada 1916–22* Galerie de l'Institut, Paris, 1957

Huelsenbeck, Richard *Dada: eine literarische Dokumentation* Rewohlt Verlag, Hamburg, 1964

Mehring, Walter *Berlin Dada* Verlag die Arche, Zürich, 1959

Motherwell, Robert (editor) *Dada Painters and Poets: An Anthology* Wittenborn, Schultz Inc., New York, 1951

Pierre, José *Le Futurisme et le Dadaisme* Editions Rencontre, Lausanne, 1967

Richter, Hans *Dada, art and anti-art* Thames and Hudson, London, 1965; McGraw–Hill, New York, 1966

Rubin, William S. *Dada, Surrealism and their Heritage* W.H.Allen, London, 1968; Museum of Modern Art, New York, 1968

Verkauf, Willy (editor) *Dada: Monograph of a Monument* George Wittenborn, New York, 1957

# Index

*Italicized numbers refer to illustrations*

# STUDIO VISTA | DUTTON PICTUREBACKS

**edited by David Herbert**

**British churches** by Edwin Smith and Olive Cook
**European domestic architecture** by Sherban Cantacuzino
**Great modern architecture** by Sherban Cantacuzino
**Modern churches of the world** by Robert Maguire and Keith Murray
**Modern houses of the world** by Sherban Cantacuzino

---

**African sculpture** by William Fagg and Margaret Plass
**European sculpture** by David Bindman
**Florentine sculpture** by Anthony Bertram
**Greek sculpture** by John Barron
**Indian sculpture** by Philip Rawson
**Michelangelo** by Anthony Bertram
**Modern sculpture** by Alan Bowness

---

**Art deco** by Bevis Hillier
**Art nouveau** by Mario Amaya
**The Bauhaus** by Gillian Naylor
**Cartoons and caricatures** by Bevis Hillier
**Dada** by Kenneth Coutts-Smith
**De Stijl** by Paul Overy
**Modern graphics** by Keith Murgatroyd
**Modern prints** by Pat Gilmour
**Pop art: object and image** by Christopher Finch
**The Pre-Raphaelites** by John Nicoll
**Surrealism** by Roger Cardinal and Robert Stuart Short
**1000 years of drawing** by Anthony Bertram

---

**Arms and armour** by Howard L. Blackmore
**The art of the garden** by Miles Hadfield
**Art in silver and gold** by Gerald Taylor
**Costume in pictures** by Phillis Cunnington
**Firearms** by Howard L. Blackmore
**Jewelry** by Graham Hughes
**Modern ballet** by John Percival
**Modern ceramics** by Geoffrey Beard
**Modern furniture** by Ella Moody
**Modern glass** by Geoffrey Beard
**Motoring history** by L. T. C. Rolt
**Railway history** by C. Hamilton Ellis
**Toys** by Patrick Murray

---

**Charlie Chaplin: early comedies** by Isabel Quigly
**The films of Alfred Hitchcock** by George Perry
**French film** by Roy Armes
**The great funnies** by David Robinson
**Greta Garbo** by Raymond Durgnat and John Kobal
**Marlene Dietrich** by John Kobal
**Movie monsters** by Denis Gifford
**New cinema in Britain** by Roger Manvell
**New cinema in Europe** by Roger Manvell
**New cinema in the USA** by Roger Manvell
**The silent cinema** by Liam O'Leary